Library of Congress Cataloging-in-Publication Data

Kisseloff, Jeff.
  Who is baseball's greatest pitcher? / Jeff Kisseloff.– 1st ed.
      p. cm.
"A Marcato book."
Summary: Asks the reader to compare the statistics for thirty-three of
baseball's greatest starting pitchers and decide who is the best.
Includes bibliographical references (p. 178).
ISBN 0-8126-2685-0 (cloth: alk. paper)
1. Pitchers (Baseball)–United States–Biography–Juvenile literature.
2. Pitchers (Baseball)–Rating of–United States–Juvenile literature.
[1. Baseball players.] I. Title.
GV865.A1K555 2003
796.359'092'2–dc21

                                                        2003001245

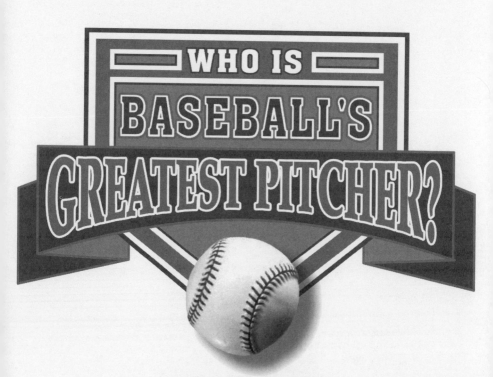

WHO IS
BASEBALL'S
GREATEST PITCHER?

Jeff Kisseloff

Cricket Books
A Marcato Book
Chicago

Contents ....

When I was growing up, my brother, Alan, and I invented a two-person baseball game we called grounders that we played for hours. We played stickball and stoop ball, "catch flies up," and pitchers and catchers. We learned how much fun you can have inside with a table leg and a tennis ball on a Saturday night when your parents aren't home. We flipped baseball cards, watched baseball, argued baseball, and, with our parents (who love the game as much as we do), went to baseball games as often as we could.

I would never have written this book without Alan's influence, so this book is dedicated to him with love and thanks.

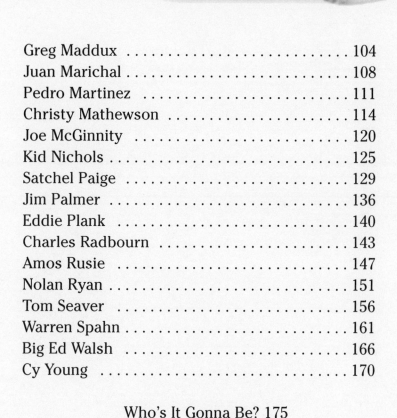

Let's Talk Pitching

This book was written in the modest hope that one day you might use it to change the world.

Hey, it could happen.

Let's say you find yourself on *Jeopardy,* and the final question in the annual Tournament of Champions is, "He was the last pitcher to win forty games in a season." Because you've read this book, you're the only one to correctly answer, "Who was Big Ed Walsh?" You win a million dollars. You parlay your money and newfound fame into a political career. You're elected to the House of Representatives and then the Senate and eventually you become president of the United States. Now you're basically running the whole world. You can make peace. You can declare war. You can make MTV required viewing in school.

You the man (or the woman)!

But wait—it gets even better. Once you're president, you can make your own rules. You can eat what you want. You don't have to have a bedtime. Every famous person in the world wants to meet you, which means you have this great social life. Best of all, your parents can no longer tell you what to do because you can just say, "Hey, I'm the president," and then make them ambassadors to some far-off place and take away their cell phone privileges so they can't keep bugging you.

And it all started here.

Now, on the off chance that this book does not have a major impact on world affairs, it may have another, let's say, more immediately attainable goal. First, I'm going to let you in on a little secret: There's more going on here than just baseball stats.

As someone who can recite all of Sandy Koufax's life-time numbers by heart, I'm not going to tell you that isn't vital knowledge. Of course it is. And this book really *is* about comparing Cy Young's 511 wins to Nolan Ryan's 5,714 strikeouts to figure out who is the best. But let's say you're at a party and someone has lifted a pack of cigarettes from the local deli. He's offering them around the room. The supposedly cool kids each take a cigarette. Do you? You weigh the options and the possible consequences and decide. That's what this book is really about: sharpening your ability to weigh options. (Anyone who decided to light up, please see me after class.)

You may not realize it, but from the time you wake up until the time you go to sleep, you're constantly making choices. They're not always life-and-death decisions, but the option you select will have a decided impact on your life, whether it's for only that moment or the next month, for the next year or the next 10 years.

Think about it. Your alarm clock rings. It's 6:30 A.M. on a school day. Do you throw the clock against the wall and go back to sleep, or do you drag yourself out of bed and get dressed? If you get up, you lose sleep—but you get to school on time. You might learn something, and your parents and teachers will continue to operate under the impression that you're a good kid. If you stay in bed, you might get some more sleep—but you also risk the wrath of your parents, teachers, and the bully who sits next to you who was expecting to cheat off you during today's quiz. So you have a choice. You weigh the options and decide.

Once you wake up, you sort through the pile of clothes on the floor by your bed. Will it be the baggy jeans, or will you play it safe with the dress-code police? Do you brush your teeth or risk offending everyone you breathe on? Is it going to be Cheerios or the sugary Cocoa Puffs? You haven't even gotten out of the house yet and already you've had to weigh the benefits and drawbacks of a host of choices. And those are the easy ones. Sometimes the options facing you will be more serious ones—much more serious. There will almost certainly be choices presented to you in the next few years when a wrong decision could end your life prematurely. One of the reasons why I am writing this book is that when I was in school I had friends who made wrong choices and didn't survive.

If this book can help you spot the right choices more easily, if it makes you laugh and tells you a few things about our national pastime that you didn't know before, if it inspires you to read further about some of the people mentioned in these pages, if you can relate their lives in some way to your own, then this book will have done its job.

But let's talk baseball, shall we? Or more specifically, pitching.

If the ballpark is a castle, the throne is a 24-inch-long piece of rubber set into a mound of dirt 10 inches higher than the rest of the field. Perched on the throne is the pitcher. Surrounding him are his eight loyal subjects, who are ready to sacrifice their bodies, if necessary, to preserve their leader's reign. Of course, there are limits to their loyalty. A poorly performing monarch will be deposed quickly and sent to the guillotine. His successor is chosen from a group of princes who wait to be summoned to the throne from a special courtyard called the bull pen. Once the new king is anointed, he is greeted by his hopeful subjects with pats on his royal rump. Then they return to their manors, or positions, and the new reign begins. Long live the king! May he rule many an inning!

Come to think of it, baseball is a very egalitarian monarchy, meaning that anyone can be king, from a lowly serf with a 6.00 earned run average to a lordly Cy Young Award winner. But the reason the pitcher is king (the king of diamonds!) is that he controls all the action on the field. Every baseball game ever played has always started the same way—with the ball in the pitcher's hand. Although the rules about what he can do with that ball and how he can do it have changed, the pitcher will always remain the most important figure on the baseball diamond, because he controls the baseball. How well he controls it determines the outcome of the contest. Will it be a weapon in his hand, or will it be used as a weapon against him? That's the ultimate question.

When the rules of baseball were first laid out by Alexander Cartwright in 1845, he put very severe restrictions on the pitcher—so severe, in fact, that the pitcher was hardly a king at all. He was more like a slave, forced by law to toss the ball underhand wherever the batter wanted it, as if he were pitching in a softball game at a July 4th picnic. If the batter didn't like the pitch, he didn't have to swing. Since there were no called strikes, the hitter could just stand there until he got the pitch he wanted. The only thing that was supposed to prevent this from happening was the "gentlemanly code" of conduct, which said that players would not unnecessarily delay the game.

So much for good intentions: In one game in the 1850s, a pitcher named Al Smith served up 54 pitches

before the obviously ungentlemanly batter found one to his liking.

There were also no walks. But to really make things worse for the pitcher, he was forced to soft toss from a box in the middle of the diamond, which was only 45 feet from home plate. He wasn't a pitcher; he was target practice.

Life was pretty bleak for the poor moundsman . . . until a savior came along in the form of a teenager named Jim Creighton. Playing for the New York Excelsiors in 1860, the 17-year-old Creighton was the first pitcher to put some speed on the ball. He also put spin on it by flicking his wrist just before releasing it. The poor hitters were helpless.

It figures that it was some smart aleck kid who would break the rules. But instead of suspending his horse-and-buggy license, the umpires let him get away with it. They recognized he was good for the game, since he gave it some competitive balance. He was also good for their tootsies, because when Creighton was on the mound, the umpires weren't standing up for six hours at a time.

Called balls and strikes were introduced in 1864. In 1870, the National Association of Professional Base Ball Players was formed, and with it came a few more rule changes. Batters could now call for a high (waist to shoulders) or low (waist to knees) pitch, basically creating two strike zones. To speed up the game, a walk was awarded when nine pitches missed either of the zones. Although pitchers were still forced to use a straight-arm, underhand delivery, they could legally snap their wrists to produce a spin.

That's where Arthur "Candy" Cummings comes in. Cummings was tossing some clamshells on the beach in the 1860s when he discovered that by snapping his wrist sharply just before he released the shells he could make them curve. Candy tried it out on a baseball and discovered a sweet pitch. Even though he weighed barely 120 pounds, he became a superstar. Too bad he couldn't patent his discovery, because soon every crafty (or "dodgy") pitcher had a curve ball in his repertoire, and suddenly pitchers were getting respect.

In 1880, eight balls, rather than nine, became a walk. The next year, the number was reduced to seven. By 1884, the waist-high rule was being ignored so often that it was tossed out, and pitchers could now legally use a shoulder-high delivery.

The pitcher's mound still hadn't been invented. Instead, pitchers threw from a box in the middle of the diamond. The box (now you know where the phrase "back through the box" comes from) was 6 feet long and 6 feet wide. It did offer the pitcher some advantages. The rules stated that the pitcher had to begin his motion from the back line, but there was nothing that prevented him from using a running start, jumping in the air, or standing on his head if he wanted to, just as long as he stayed within the confines of the box.

Pitchers were always looking for an edge anywhere they could get it, and many of them learned they could use the width of the box to their advantage. Starting their delivery on the far left or right of the box gave them a sharp angle to the plate. Of course, once they got good at that, the rule makers took it away from them in an effort to beef up the offense. This would happen throughout baseball history, as the rule makers time and again sought to make it easier for hitters: They felt a 10-9 slugfest drew more fans to the park than a 1-0 pitchers' duel. What the rule makers did in 1881 was move the box back to 50 feet from home plate. That not only cut down on the pitcher's speed but also reduced the advantage the pitcher gained by pitching from the edge of the box.

After 1886, a hitter could no longer tell the pitcher where he wanted the ball. (Of course, they could still ask politely, but the pitcher would usually respond by telling the hitter where he could put it.) Instead, a strike zone was created between the top of the shoulder and the bottom of the knee. A batter was called out after four strikes, and a walk was now five balls. In 1888, it became three strikes and you're out, and the next year a walk was set where it is today—four balls.

The next major change occurred in 1893, when, owing mostly to the frightening fastball of Amos Rusie, "The Hoosier Thunderbolt," the pitching mound was moved back to its current distance—60 feet 6 inches from home plate. It also became a mound instead of a box. At the center of the mound was a rubber slab that was a foot long and six inches wide. Two years later, the slab was enlarged to its present-day 24 inches by 6 inches. The pitcher now began his motion with his foot touching the rubber. He could no longer take a running start before delivering the ball to the plate. Pitchers did get a rare boost in 1896 when they were no longer required to hold the ball in plain view. That made it easier for them to use their motion to fool the hitters.

As pitchers continued to experiment in their search for any advantage, pitching became more of a scientific process. Pitchers learned that by altering their grip they could make the ball drop or rise, move in on hitters or move away from them. The basic curve was called the "drop ball," and its variations were called "inshoots" and "outshoots."

Pitchers also learned that by applying various substances to the ball, such as saliva or mud, they could make it behave in unpredictable ways. They found that scuffing a ball with a sharp object or a piece of emery paper cleverly hidden in a glove or pocket would also make it veer off course. Discoloring the ball with tobacco juice was especially effective when games stretched into twilight time (major league games weren't played under the lights until 1939), because a brown ball was hard to see. Often in those days, only one ball was used in a game, and since both teams had to hit the discolored ball, the pitcher had better make sure his team was ahead before painting the cowhide with the brown stuff.

Other pitches that were developed in the 19th century included the change of pace and the knuckle ball, which was delivered in a way that stopped the ball from spinning. That allowed it to ride the air currents up and down, like a theme-park ride. The knuckler was not only hard to control, it was also nearly impossible to catch. Finally, in the 1960s, a larger catcher's mitt was developed specifically for catching knuckle balls. Bob Uecker, a former catcher, was once asked his secret for catching the knuckle ball. It was simple, he said. "I just wait for it to stop rolling and then I pick it up."

In the early 1900s, the New York Giants' Rube Marquard developed an effective pitch he called the "turkey trot." It resembled today's forkball. He gripped the baseball with his index and middle fingers spread around the edges. After it was released, the ball broke downward, with the result that hitters swung over it.

A forward-thinking player named Crazy Schmit, who played in the 1890s, is generally credited with being the first pitcher to literally keep a book on hitters, which was not a crazy idea at all. It obviously didn't help him, because he didn't last long in the majors. (Maybe he couldn't read his own handwriting.) But ever since then, pitchers and managers have followed his lead to the extent that not only do teams keep heavy notebooks filled with information on opposing hitters, but now computers and videos are used to track hitters' strengths and weaknesses.

Pitchers also learned to conserve their strength so they could still be effective in the later innings and vary their pitches to keep hitters off balance. They also found out they could intimidate hitters by throwing at them every once in a while. Since hitters didn't wear batting helmets, bean balls were often an effective—and dangerous—weapon in the pitcher's arsenal.

The pitcher's best friend in the early days of baseball was probably the ball itself. The period from 1900 to 1920 is known as the Dead Ball Era. It was a golden age for pitchers—runners crossed home so infrequently you'd think they had a moat around the plate. In the Dead Ball Era, even an average pitcher could have a 2.50 ERA. Today, that would qualify him for the Cy Young Award.

In the Dead Ball Era, pitchers didn't have to worry about throwing a perfect pitch every time. Today, you throw Barry Bonds a fastball an inch from where you want it and he's liable to send it into McCovey Cove. In those days, there was more room for mistakes so a pitcher could save his strength for the few key pitches that might determine the outcome of the game.

The primary reason for this was the ball. Most games were played with only one. If a foul was hit into the stands, a poor usher had to risk life and limb by chasing after the person who caught it and prying it loose from his fingers. After a couple of innings of being pounded by baseball bats, the ball was as squishy as a rotten orange. You want to know why Fred Odwell led the National League with nine home runs in 1905? Get an orange and see how far you can hit it with a bat.

The ball would not only soften, it would also become discolored by a combination of dirt, spit, tobacco, and whatever else it came in contact with. Beginning in 1920, in an effort to jump-start offenses, umpires were instructed to use only fresh baseballs. Pitchers, of course, were heartbroken, but hitters and ushers danced with joy.

Batters were given another boost when spitballs were banned the same year. Well, not quite banned. Pitchers who primarily threw the spitball were permitted to load up on the ball until they retired. Over the next 14 years, the number of spitballers gradually dried up. In case you're interested, the last ball that was legally "loogied" was thrown by Burleigh Grimes of the Yankees in 1934. I'd like to report that with Grimes's last pitch there wasn't a dry eye in the house, but I doubt he put that much moisture on the ball.

Of course, Grimes only threw the last *legal* spitball. Pitchers continue to throw it—they've just learned to hide it. But they've also picked up many new, effective ways of maintaining their mastery over batters—remember, even the best hitters succeed in getting a hit only 33 percent of the time. The slider looks like a fastball but darts off as it crosses the plate. It appeared in various forms early in the 20th century, but it wasn't until after World War II that it became very popular. Many baseball historians believe the popularity of the slider is the number-one reason why batting averages have dropped so steeply in the last 50 years.

An even more devastating pitch is the split-fingered fastball. Although some people claim it was first thrown more than 50 years ago, the splitter was popularized by reliever Bruce Sutter in the 1970s. The splitter is thrown like Rube Marquard's turkey trot, but faster. The reason it's so effective is that it looks like a fastball until the last second, when it just drops, as if it were falling off a table. Hitters are still trying to figure out the splitter, which has turned some very ordinary pitchers into millionaires.

Two other developments have altered the lives of modern-day pitchers. The first is the increasing reliance on relief pitchers. When baseball began, there were no relievers. Players could be substituted only when there was an injury, and if someone was brought in to pitch relief, he was already in the game—he just switched positions with the pitcher. That changed in 1891, when bench substitutes were allowed for the first time. Still, bull pens were not exactly hotbeds of activity. Starters completed most of their games, even if they were getting blown out. The New York Giants' crafty manager John McGraw was always years ahead of his time. He was the first to use a regular reliever—Doc Crandall—although Crandall frequently appeared as a starter as well. Usually, if a team needed a reliever, one of its starters was pressed into service on his day off. Even the best pitchers helped out. Lefty Grove, one of the greatest pitchers of all time, earned 55 saves in his career.

Firpo Marberry of the Washington Senators was one of the first relief specialists. In 1925, he appeared in 55 games and started none of them. He led the league in saves three years in a row from 1924 to 1926, although he didn't know it at the time. The statistic wasn't invented until 1960, when sportswriter Jerome Holtzman examined Pittsburgh reliever Elroy Face's 18-1 record in 1959 and determined he hadn't had a very good year because many of his wins occurred after he gave up the team's lead. Holtzman then created "the save," giving a reliever credit for one when he finished a game successfully after entering it with either the potential tying or winning run on base or at the plate. Later, a save was awarded when a relief pitcher protected a two-run lead. Now it's even easier to earn a save. A pitcher protecting a lead of up to three runs can earn a save.

The image of the modern-day closer, swaggering in from the bull pen to finish out a game with his jacket slung over his shoulder, began with "Fireman" Joe Page of the Yankees in the 1940s. With Page, relief pitching really came into its own. Probably the clearest sign of its acceptance as a legitimate occupation came in 1950, when reliever Jim Konstanty of the Philadelphia Phillies won the National League MVP.

Since then, a number of relief pitchers have won the Cy Young Award, although it's pretty much limited to closers. Long relievers and set-up men, who don't have such obvious statistics to measure their value, still don't get much respect. "A lot of long relievers are ashamed to tell their parents what they do," said former pitcher Jim Bouton, who wrote a very funny book about baseball called *Ball Four*. "The only nice thing about it is you get to wear a uniform like everybody else."

Relief pitchers may be underappreciated as a group, but they do get a lot of work. In the 1940s and 1950s, a starter like Bob Feller was still completing a third to a half of his starts. In the 1960s, Sandy Koufax's percentage of complete games was more than half. But today's pitchers have a different attitude. The last year that Roger Clemens pitched more than 10 complete games in a season was 1992. The leader in complete games in 2002 was Randy Johnson with 8.

That means when a pitcher takes the mound to start a game, he does so with a different mind-set than a hurler of 100 years ago. He doesn't really have to conserve his strength, because he knows that the team will have its set-up men and closer ready to begin their workday around the seventh inning. And if a team has a great bull pen, the starter knows he just has to go five to get the win. If the trend continues, 30 years from now a starting pitcher will probably last an average of a third of an inning before the manager goes to his bull pen.

The other major development is mostly not so good for pitchers. That is the introduction of the designated hitter in the American League in 1973. It's bad because it means the pitcher has another tough bat to face in the lineup instead of an easy out in the number-nine slot— usually the opposing pitcher.

Pitchers do benefit from the DH, though. Remember the big controversy after Roger Clemens beaned Mike Piazza in 2000? If Clemens had been pitching in the National League and was still in the game an inning or two later, chances are the Mets' pitcher would have bounced a fastball off his rib cage, if not his noggin, in retaliation. But the DH rule let Clemens off the hook. Pitchers can be pretty tough as long as they can hide in the dugout when it otherwise would be their turn to bat.

So Who's the Best?

From the hundreds of pitchers who have taken the mound in major league history, I've winnowed the choices down to 33. That doesn't mean if there is a pitcher you think should be included you can't jot down some of his stats and compare him to the others. Actually, that's a great idea. If you have a favorite, take a look at his record, learn about his achievements, and then see how he stacks up against the others.

There are plenty of wonderful pitchers who didn't make the final cut. Look up Mickey Welch, one of baseball's earliest stars, who won over 300 games in the 19th century. Check out Rube Waddell's amazing strikeout marks or Robin Robert's run in the 1950s when he was baseball's winningest pitcher. Ferguson Jenkins, who won 284 games while pitching for some very average teams, also came close. I found, though, that for each pitcher who was included, I could make an argument why *he* is the best. For one reason or another, I didn't feel I could do that with those I left out. If you disagree, great! The endless room for discussion is a big part of what makes baseball so wonderful.

You will notice that of the 33 pitchers on my list, none are relief specialists. I have nothing against relievers. Let

me assure you that some of my best friends are relief pitchers. But on a practical basis, I just don't think you can compare someone who goes one or two innings with someone who goes six or eight or nine. Only rarely does a closer work 100 innings in a year. A good starter these days works over 200 innings. A hundred years ago, they went 300 to 400.

Mariano Rivera is an amazing closer, but the most he's ever worked in a season is 108 innings. If he had to go even five innings in one game, his arm might fall off. Or if he had to take some speed off his heater to last a whole game, he would be that much more hittable. Baseball history shows that many great starters, such as Lefty Grove and Three Finger Brown, made terrific relievers, but it doesn't work the other way around.

The Yankees' former closer Sparky Lyle said about relief pitching: "Why pitch nine innings when you can get just as famous pitching two?" He's right in a way, but that's also why he doesn't get to be included here.

Each year, baseball historians invent new statistics to more accurately measure the relative worth of a player. I'm sure they are very useful, but the formulas they come up with are sometimes so complex that they would have Einstein scratching his head. I have to confess something here: I failed trigonometry in high school. When it comes to math, I'm a blithering idiot. Out of sympathy for my brothers and sisters who suffer from "mathitis" along with me, I've tried to keep things simple by using numbers that are easily comparable. These are the kinds of statistics that you find on the backs of baseball cards. Still, it's important to remember that even the simplest numbers have many different factors that go into them. That's what makes for so many differences of opinion.

Let's look at them:

Won-lost record—How many games did he win, and how many did he lose? The best pitchers win many more games than they lose, but sometimes a great pitcher plays for a terrible team. He might pitch a great game but lose 1-0. You don't see that reflected in his record. Winning percentage is a way of putting a single number to a won-lost record. You can figure it out by taking the pitcher's wins and dividing it by his total wins and losses. For example, if a pitcher has a 9-5 record, you would divide 9 by 14 and determine the pitcher has a winning percentage of .643, if you round the third number up. Most pitchers would be very happy with that. But is it good enough to be the greatest?

Earned run average (ERA)—Some people feel this is the most important pitching statistic. An earned run average is the average number of runs that a pitcher gives up per nine innings of play. It's an easy statistic to determine. First, find the average number of runs the pitcher gave up per inning. For example, if he pitched 40 innings and gave up 6 runs, divide 6 by 40 and get .15. Then, to get the average number per nine innings, multiply .15 by 9 to get 1.35—an excellent ERA. For many years, pitchers had to have an ERA under 2.00 to be in contention for the ERA crown. That number has since gone way up. Nowadays anything under 4.00 is considered worthy of a multimillion-dollar contract. There are any number of reasons for this, including smaller ballparks, a livelier ball, better trained hitters, and the possible use of performance-enhancing drugs by hitters. It's up to you to determine why. Is it for those reasons, or is it because there were better pitchers back then?

Games, Games started, Complete games, Innings pitched—Again, there are reasons for everything in baseball (as in life!), but in the case of these figures, it's a matter of the higher the better. A pitcher who appears in many games is probably one of the best pitchers on the staff. Workhorse pitchers throw more innings, which is very important to a team. If a pitcher has more complete games than other pitchers, that indicates he is strong enough to finish what he starts and that he frequently pitches well enough to still be in the game at the end. Remember, though, that in the 19th century the percentage of complete games was very, very high. Was it because pitchers back then were tougher than today's pitchers?

Strikeouts, Walks—You want more of the first and less of the second, but not every great pitcher is a strike-out pitcher, and just because a pitcher gives up a lot of walks doesn't mean he isn't an overwhelming performer. Also, hitters tend to swing for the fences today much more than they did 100 years ago, so strikeouts were a much greater accomplishment back then. Think about that when you compare Rube Waddell's 349 strikeouts in 1904 to Randy Johnson's 347 in 2000.

Hits, Runs—You want to see less of these in a pitcher's record, although many excellent pitchers understood that they could afford to give up a few hits if it meant conserving their strength—as long as they didn't allow the runners to score. The best pitchers succeeded in that strategy, and it was a smart one, because if it worked, it meant they could pitch longer while also helping the team.

Shutouts—You have to pitch a full nine innings and allow no runs to get credit for a shutout. Obviously, this is a great indication of all-around pitching excellence because of all the difficult challenges that must be surmounted to pitch a shutout.

There are many other factors to consider when trying to decide who is the best. The number of no-hitters, if any, a pitcher threw, is one example. Also, what is the pitcher's record under pressure, either down the stretch of a pennant drive or in the World Series? Is he the guy leading the team when it counts the most? The best usually are.

What about awards? Did he win the Cy Young Award or the MVP? Was he elected to the all-star game (after 1933, when the all-star game began)? The honors a pitcher receives are an excellent indication of value.

Here's something else to think about: left-handers vs. right-handers. You might think they're equal, but if you're a lefty, I've got bad news for you. Southpaws, as lefties are sometimes called (in the 1880s, a Chicago sportswriter named Finley Peter Dunne coined the term because when a lefty was on the mound his arm faced the south side), are definitely at a disadvantage in baseball. Why? I'll let you think about that one for a minute. . . .

Figured it out yet?

Here's the answer: When a right-handed hitter faces a right-handed pitcher, he has a much harder time seeing the ball because it's hidden by the pitcher's body. Also, if the pitcher throws with a sidearm motion, the ball will arrive at the plate from an angle that makes it very hard to hit. Left-handed hitters face the same problem against left-handed pitchers. The reason why righty pitchers have an advantage over their southpaw brothers is simply a matter of numbers. There are many more right-handed hitters in baseball (and right-handers in life)! For a left-hander, it's like running a race with weights tied to your legs. You need to consider this when measuring the career of, let's say, Sandy Koufax against that of Walter Johnson, and give Koufax and other lefties a little extra credit for their accomplishments.

Another factor that may weigh on a pitcher's record is the size of his home ballpark. Especially in the early 20th century, there was great variation in the size of stadiums from city to city. Back then, you had ballparks that were so small that if you stood on home plate and stretched on your tippy toes, you could drop a nickel over the center-field fence. But you also had ballparks in which the center-field bleachers were so far from home that the people sitting out there were in a different zip code. An easy fly ball in the old Polo Grounds was a home run in Philadelphia's Baker Bowl. That is often reflected in the home pitcher's statistics, so while making your decision you might want to do some research into the pitchers' home parks. What you find may influence your choice.

So where did I get my statistics? I invented 'em. Just kidding. Actually, my main source was the tenth edition of *The Baseball Encyclopedia.* For additional numbers that weren't in the *Encyclopedia*, I chose the seventh edition of *Total Baseball.* Those two books don't always agree. In fact, there are a lot of stats that are in dispute, especially from baseball's earliest days because recordkeeping was so poor back then. Baseball historians continue to comb through old newspapers and files to straighten out those stats. As a result, they seem to change as often as the weather. Did Old Hoss Radbourn win 59 games or 60 in 1884? The *Encyclopedia* says 60. *Total Baseball* says 59. Who is right? Since there will always be disagreement, I've just tried to stay consistent and stick with one source, so this book says 60.

You've got a real challenge ahead of you when comparing players from different eras. Balls were manufactured differently in the early 20th century. They're wound more tightly now, which means they travel farther. Fielders had much smaller gloves up through the 1950s and 1960s.

Casey Stengel once complained about the new larger mitts: "They're not gloves, they're appliances." Bigger gloves mean better defense (in most cases). If Walter Johnson's fielders had had bigger gloves, that might have meant a few more wins for "The Big Train."

Today's players are probably better nourished than players were 50 years ago. Many train during the off-season now. Players didn't do that so much years ago. Salaries were so low, they had to find additional work. Players now also have access to technology, such as video cameras, computers, and hitting machines, that wasn't available 20 years ago. Current players also have access to surgical advances and rehabilitation techniques that weren't available even 20 years ago. Injuries that almost certainly forced a pitcher into early retirement can now be overcome in less than a season.

There's also an interesting question about the level of play today as compared to that before World War II. On one hand, there are many players today who probably wouldn't have been in the majors before each league expanded from 8 to 10 teams in the 1960s. (There are now 30 teams in all.) With more slots available, lower-quality players are filling out many rosters. That means a lot of teams have some easy outs in their lineups.

On the other hand, baseball was closed to all black and Latino players before World War II. This was a crime and a tragedy. Many Negro League players would have been superstars in the major leagues. Pitchers who played in the majors before 1947 didn't have to face those great players, while today's pitchers are battling against everyone who has the athletic ability to play. That includes not only African American players but also players from many other countries around the world. Baseball is a much more inclusive sport than it was 50 years ago, and every-body—fans and athletes alike—is much richer for it.

So, are you ready? The 33 pitchers are in alphabetical order. After that, you'll find a list of books you might enjoy that will help you do additional research, if you want. There are also a few more questions for you to ponder. But don't look for me to tell you who is the best. That's for you to decide. So what are you waiting for? Turn the page and start digging in.

Grover Cleveland Alexander
(Alex, Pete, Old Pete)

b. February 26, 1887, Elba, Nebraska
d. November 4, 1950, St. Paul, Nebraska
Career: 1911–1930
Record: 373-208
Right-handed

This was the scene on October 10, 1926, when some 38,000 fans at Yankee Stadium witnessed the most electrifying confrontation in World Series history.

It's the seventh inning of Game 7 between the St. Louis Cardinals and the New York Yankees. St. Louis is up, 3-2, but the Bombers have loaded the bases with two outs. At the plate is hotshot rookie Tony Lazzeri, who is second in R.B.I. to Babe Ruth. In from the bull pen comes the Cardinals' 39-year-old Grover Cleveland Alexander, once the game's finest pitcher but now in the sunset of his career. Alexander had pitched a complete-game victory the day before. Would the aging veteran have enough left in his right arm to somehow vanquish the rookie and keep the Cardinals' championship hopes alive?

They make movies out of this stuff. Come to think of it, they did. Baseball historian Bill James points out that Grover Cleveland Alexander was the only major league player to be named after one U.S. president and portrayed on film by another. The 1952 movie of Alex's life was called *The Winning Team,* and the actor was none other than Ronald Reagan, whose own winning team sent him to the White House in 1980.

So what happened that day? Let's talk a little more about Alex first.

ained an advantage by throwing both his fastball and
rve at a number of different speeds. As if that wasn't
ough, in 1920, with the onset of the livelier ball, he
apted by developing a screwball, which was then called
fadeaway."(We'll talk at length about the "fadeaway" in
e chapter on Christy Mathewson.)

He was also a quick worker. Most of his games were
er in an hour and a half. "He had such an effortless motion,
fastball sneaked by you," said Hall of Famer Frankie
ch, who batted against Alexander many times. "You'd
set, but it would be by you in the catcher's mitt. He
ed his pitches like nobody before or since, and if you
d to guess with him, you were a cinch to lose."

Despite his brilliance, Pete was traded by Philadelphia
hicago after the 1917 season because the Phillies knew
as about to be drafted into World War I. He spent several
ths at the front line, seeing action in some of the worst
es of the war. All you have to do is compare photo-
s of Pete in 1911 and in 1919 to see how dramatically
wful experience aged him. He began drinking heavily
the war, when he began suffering from headaches
d by being so close to cannon fire. He also became
tic, which might have had its roots in the beaning
eived back in 1909. He never would talk about what
ned in Europe, but war takes a psychological toll on
he strongest of people, and Pete was no exception.
t that he was ineffective when he returned. Pete won
es in 1920 and 22 in 1923. He was traded to the
ls in 1926. They won the pennant that year, with "Old
inning several key contests down the stretch. That's
found himself pitching in relief in Game 7 of the World
after already winning his starts in Games 2 and 6.
you do it?" asked his manager, Roger Hornsby,
anding Pete the ball.

It wasn't that his parents were such great fans of the
country's 22nd (and 24th) president when he was born—
it was just that they already had 11 kids and they had run
out of names.

Young Grover was nicknamed "Dode." Like most farm
boys, he was assigned chores. One of them was pulling
potatoes out of the ground, but instead of searching for
spuds, Alex preferred throwing rocks at selected targets,
such as the clothespins hanging on his neighbor's laundry
line. Soon his aim was so accurate that when he was sent
out to catch a chicken or turkey for the family dinner, he
didn't bother running after it.

"Dode could pick them off with rocks while they were
running around outside the henhouse," his mother
recalled years later.

No wonder he became such a great control pitcher. Over
the course of his career, Alexander averaged 1.6 walks per nine
innings, the same as Christy Mathewson, the Dead Ball Era's
other great control pitcher. Like Satchel Paige years later, Alex
loved to showcase his accuracy. He would have his catcher
sit behind home plate, holding out a tomato can. Alex
would toss one ball after another right into the can.

Despite his great control, Alexander was not regarded
with interest by most teams because of a nearly fatal accident
he suffered on the field during a minor league game. He
was running to second base when the shortstop's throw
hit him smack in the head. Alex collapsed in a heap and
began choking on the blood pouring down his throat.
Only quick action by another player saved his life. He was
unconscious for a week and he suffered from double
vision for months. After that, the Phillies were the only
team to take a chance on him. They signed him for $500,
which turned out to be a real bargain.

In spring training of 1911, Alex was limited to pitching batting practice. Still, he caught the eye of catcher Pat Moran, who quickly recognized the rookie's extraordinary ability. Moran couldn't persuade manager Red Dooin to put Alex in an actual game, though, until finally Dooin got tired of being nagged. To shut his catcher up, he penciled Alex in to pitch in an exhibition game against the world champion A's. "You'll pitch five innings, and they'll be murder, but at least you'll learn something," Dooin told Alex. Instead, it was Dooin and the A's who got a lesson. Pitching with an easy, economical, three-quarters motion that disguised a hopping fastball, Alex threw five innings of no-hit, no-run ball.

The rookie became the ace of the staff in record time, literally. His league-leading 28 wins that season are still the highest total ever for a rookie since 1900. He was also first in complete games, tied for first in shutouts, and second in strikeouts. His 2.57 ERA was fifth best. Not bad for a kid no one wanted!

Those numbers are all the more remarkable in light of the fact that the Phillies' home park, Baker Bowl, was a nightmare for pitchers. The right-field wall was only 272 feet from home plate. Right-center was 320 feet away. (Your little sister could have put one over that fence.) By comparison, at Mathewson's home turf, in the Polo Grounds, the center-field clubhouse was 483 feet out. That was so far from home plate, it almost had a different time zone.

In Baker Bowl, Alex needed his great control just to survive. But he didn't just survive—he excelled. He averaged 27 wins a year for his first seven seasons. From 1915 through 1917, he was at his peak, winning 31, 33, and 30 games, leading the league each season. Let's compare that with Mathewson at his best, when he won 30 or more three years in a row from 1903 to 1905. Both won 94

games. Alex lost 35; Matty, 34. But that's as cl
for Mathewson. Alexander had a much lowe
1.86, and a huge lead in shutouts, 34 to 15
never had more than 12 shutouts in a seasor
16 in 1916 remains the major league record

Pete had a lot more than three brillian
led the league in victories and strikeouts
only did he win five ERA crowns, but fron
1920 his highest ERA was 1.91. He was the
seven times, tying him with Walter Johns
times leading the league. Pete's 90 shut
all-time to Johnson's—but you have to w
Johnson would have had had he been f
Baker Bowl instead of roomy Griffith Sta

The magazine *Sporting Life* compare
Johnson while they were both still acti
what it had to say:

> *Alexander is a greater pitcher than*
> *opinion of this writer, because there*
> *to the Nebraskan. When in his pr*
> *unhittable because of his terrific sp*
> *fast ball was not working good Joh*
> *to hit, as he never had much of a curv*
> *other hand, has a fast ball that has a*
> *of a break to it, than that of Johnse*
> *as fast; and added to this the Net*
> *curve ball of any pitcher in the gai*
> *Alexander's wonderful control, ar*
> *just as good as any pitcher poss*
> *easy to see that the Philly star is*

Pete threw what was called
meant it was hard for batters to l

"I can try," Pete replied.

He took only three warmup pitches before motioning that he was ready. Pete knew his speed was gone, so he had to rely on his pinpoint control. He and his catcher, Bob O'Farrell, agreed to pitch Lazzeri low and away, as Lazzeri could really turn on a high pitch. The first pitch was a ball, but the second was a strike, just where they wanted it. Then on the third pitch, Alex missed his target and threw one over the center of the plate. Lazzeri jumped on it and ripped a screaming line drive toward the left-field stands. It had the distance, but at the last second it curved left and fell foul just 10 feet from the pole.

Pete and the rest of the Cardinals breathed a sigh of relief. Now the count was 1-and-2. Pete went back to the curve. It headed right toward the heart of the plate but then dipped away, as it was supposed to. Lazzeri swung hard and missed. Strike three—the crisis was over.

Pete shut down the Yankees the rest of the way. At 39, he had won two World Series games and saved another. The next year he would exceed 20 wins for the last time before he retired in 1930. Now drinking heavily and desperate for money, he told and retold the story of the historic confrontation onstage as part of a vaudeville show.

"To tell you the truth, I'm getting a little tired of striking out Lazzeri," he said just before he died, poor and alone in a rented room in Nebraska—not as tired as Tony must have been, though.

More Numbers

A workhorse, Alexander was a six-time leader in complete games and a seven-time leader in innings pitched (a major league record). He is 10th lifetime in innings pitched. He pitched four one-hitters in 1915. Before he retired, he wanted to get enough wins to surpass Mathewson's total of 372. He finally got his 373rd and last win in 1929, but baseball historians later took his lead away when they added a win to Matty's record, giving him 373 as well.

Throwing Strikes

He was by far the most dominant National League pitcher of his decade. Considering that he spent his prime in a terrible park for pitchers, his record for his first years with the Phillies is spectacular. The few players with better numbers in some categories all pitched in parks much more favorable to pitchers.

Throwing Balls

He led the league in hits allowed four times.

It wasn't that his parents were such great fans of the country's 22nd (and 24th) president when he was born—it was just that they already had 11 kids and they had run out of names.

Young Grover was nicknamed "Dode." Like most farm boys, he was assigned chores. One of them was pulling potatoes out of the ground, but instead of searching for spuds, Alex preferred throwing rocks at selected targets, such as the clothespins hanging on his neighbor's laundry line. Soon his aim was so accurate that when he was sent out to catch a chicken or turkey for the family dinner, he didn't bother running after it.

"Dode could pick them off with rocks while they were running around outside the henhouse," his mother recalled years later.

No wonder he became such a great control pitcher. Over the course of his career, Alexander averaged 1.6 walks per nine innings, the same as Christy Mathewson, the Dead Ball Era's other great control pitcher. Like Satchel Paige years later, Alex loved to showcase his accuracy. He would have his catcher sit behind home plate, holding out a tomato can. Alex would toss one ball after another right into the can.

Despite his great control, Alexander was not regarded with interest by most teams because of a nearly fatal accident he suffered on the field during a minor league game. He was running to second base when the shortstop's throw hit him smack in the head. Alex collapsed in a heap and began choking on the blood pouring down his throat. Only quick action by another player saved his life. He was unconscious for a week and he suffered from double vision for months. After that, the Phillies were the only team to take a chance on him. They signed him for $500, which turned out to be a real bargain.

In spring training of 1911, Alex was limited to pitching batting practice. Still, he caught the eye of catcher Pat Moran, who quickly recognized the rookie's extraordinary ability. Moran couldn't persuade manager Red Dooin to put Alex in an actual game, though, until finally Dooin got tired of being nagged. To shut his catcher up, he penciled Alex in to pitch in an exhibition game against the world champion A's. "You'll pitch five innings, and they'll be murder, but at least you'll learn something," Dooin told Alex. Instead, it was Dooin and the A's who got a lesson. Pitching with an easy, economical, three-quarters motion that disguised a hopping fastball, Alex threw five innings of no-hit, no-run ball.

The rookie became the ace of the staff in record time, literally. His league-leading 28 wins that season are still the highest total ever for a rookie since 1900. He was also first in complete games, tied for first in shutouts, and second in strikeouts. His 2.57 ERA was fifth best. Not bad for a kid no one wanted!

Those numbers are all the more remarkable in light of the fact that the Phillies' home park, Baker Bowl, was a nightmare for pitchers. The right-field wall was only 272 feet from home plate. Right-center was 320 feet away. (Your little sister could have put one over that fence.) By comparison, at Mathewson's home turf, in the Polo Grounds, the center-field clubhouse was 483 feet out. That was so far from home plate, it almost had a different time zone.

In Baker Bowl, Alex needed his great control just to survive. But he didn't just survive—he excelled. He averaged 27 wins a year for his first seven seasons. From 1915 through 1917, he was at his peak, winning 31, 33, and 30 games, leading the league each season. Let's compare that with Mathewson at his best, when he won 30 or more three years in a row from 1903 to 1905. Both won 94 games. Alex lost 35; Matty, 34. But that's as close as it gets for Mathewson. Alexander had a much lower ERA, 1.53 to 1.86, and a huge lead in shutouts, 34 to 15. Mathewson never had more than 12 shutouts in a season, while Pete's 16 in 1916 remains the major league record.

Pete had a lot more than three brilliant seasons. He led the league in victories and strikeouts six times. Not only did he win five ERA crowns, but from 1915 through 1920 his highest ERA was 1.91. He was the shutout leader seven times, tying him with Walter Johnson for the most times leading the league. Pete's 90 shutouts are second all-time to Johnson's—but you have to wonder how many Johnson would have had had he been forced to pitch in Baker Bowl instead of roomy Griffith Stadium.

The magazine *Sporting Life* compared Alexander and Johnson while they were both still active players. This is what it had to say:

Alexander is a greater pitcher than Johnson, in the opinion of this writer, because there is more versatility to the Nebraskan. When in his prime Johnson was unhittable because of his terrific speed, but when his fast ball was not working good Johnson was not hard to hit, as he never had much of a curve. Alexander, on the other hand, has a fast ball that has as much, if not more, of a break to it, than that of Johnson, though not quite as fast; and added to this the Nebraskan has the best curve ball of any pitcher in the game today. Add to this Alexander's wonderful control, and a slow ball that is just as good as any pitcher possesses, and it will be easy to see that the Philly star is the king of pitchers.

Pete threw what was called a "heavy ball," which meant it was hard for batters to loft it into the air. He also gained an advantage by throwing both his fastball and curve at a number of different speeds. As if that wasn't enough, in 1920, with the onset of the livelier ball, he adapted by developing a screwball, which was then called a "fadeaway."(We'll talk at length about the "fadeaway" in the chapter on Christy Mathewson.)

He was also a quick worker. Most of his games were over in an hour and a half. "He had such an effortless motion, his fastball sneaked by you," said Hall of Famer Frankie Frisch, who batted against Alexander many times. "You'd get set, but it would be by you in the catcher's mitt. He mixed his pitches like nobody before or since, and if you tried to guess with him, you were a cinch to lose."

Despite his brilliance, Pete was traded by Philadelphia to Chicago after the 1917 season because the Phillies knew he was about to be drafted into World War I. He spent several months at the front line, seeing action in some of the worst battles of the war. All you have to do is compare photographs of Pete in 1911 and in 1919 to see how dramatically that awful experience aged him. He began drinking heavily after the war, when he began suffering from headaches caused by being so close to cannon fire. He also became epileptic, which might have had its roots in the beaning he received back in 1909. He never would talk about what happened in Europe, but war takes a psychological toll on even the strongest of people, and Pete was no exception.

Not that he was ineffective when he returned. Pete won 27 games in 1920 and 22 in 1923. He was traded to the Cardinals in 1926. They won the pennant that year, with "Old Pete" winning several key contests down the stretch. That's how he found himself pitching in relief in Game 7 of the World Series, after already winning his starts in Games 2 and 6.

"Can you do it?" asked his manager, Roger Hornsby, before handing Pete the ball.

"I can try," Pete replied.

He took only three warmup pitches before motioning that he was ready. Pete knew his speed was gone, so he had to rely on his pinpoint control. He and his catcher, Bob O'Farrell, agreed to pitch Lazzeri low and away, as Lazzeri could really turn on a high pitch. The first pitch was a ball, but the second was a strike, just where they wanted it. Then on the third pitch, Alex missed his target and threw one over the center of the plate. Lazzeri jumped on it and ripped a screaming line drive toward the left-field stands. It had the distance, but at the last second it curved left and fell foul just 10 feet from the pole.

Pete and the rest of the Cardinals breathed a sigh of relief. Now the count was 1-and-2. Pete went back to the curve. It headed right toward the heart of the plate but then dipped away, as it was supposed to. Lazzeri swung hard and missed. Strike three—the crisis was over.

Pete shut down the Yankees the rest of the way. At 39, he had won two World Series games and saved another. The next year he would exceed 20 wins for the last time before he retired in 1930. Now drinking heavily and desperate for money, he told and retold the story of the historic confrontation onstage as part of a vaudeville show.

"To tell you the truth, I'm getting a little tired of striking out Lazzeri," he said just before he died, poor and alone in a rented room in Nebraska—not as tired as Tony must have been, though.

More Numbers

A workhorse, Alexander was a six-time leader in complete games and a seven-time leader in innings pitched (a major league record). He is 10th lifetime in innings pitched. He pitched four one-hitters in 1915. Before he retired, he wanted to get enough wins to surpass Mathewson's total of 372. He finally got his 373rd and last win in 1929, but baseball historians later took his lead away when they added a win to Matty's record, giving him 373 as well.

Throwing Strikes

He was by far the most dominant National League pitcher of his decade. Considering that he spent his prime in a terrible park for pitchers, his record for his first years with the Phillies is spectacular. The few players with better numbers in some categories all pitched in parks much more favorable to pitchers.

Throwing Balls

He led the league in hits allowed four times.

Mordecai Peter Centennial Brown
(Three Finger, Miner)

b. October 19, 1876, Nyesville, Indiana
d. February 14, 1948, Terre Haute, Indiana
Career: 1903–1916
Record: 239-129
Right-handed

If this book had been called *Who Had Baseball's Greatest Nickname?* there's no doubt that Mordecai Brown would be in the top five. After all, it doesn't get much more descriptive than "Three Finger."

It could be more accurate, though. Three Finger Brown actually had parts of nine fingers. But it was the missing pieces that probably launched him on his Hall of Fame career.

When Brown was seven years old, his right hand got caught in a corn grinder on his family's farm. Doctors had to amputate nearly all of his forefinger and about half of his pinky. His middle finger was also mangled. But while he suffered terribly from his injuries, after he recovered he found they also gave him a hell of a curve ball. It was so good that Brown eventually became one of the best pitchers ever to take the mound, and his uncle's corn grinder would later become a kind of bizarre tourist attraction.

Young Mordecai had no idea at first that he could now do things with a baseball that he hadn't been able to do before. As a semipro player, he started out at third base. Then, a second accident changed his life, although this time it happened to someone else. The team's best pitcher fell and injured his shoulder. The manager asked Brown to take the mound. Very quickly, he found that if he released the ball off the stub of his index finger, it developed a very pronounced downward break. It broke so sharply that one sportswriter later said, "The only way to hit Brown's curve is with a shotgun."

Still, the sidearmer didn't make it to the major leagues until 1903, and even then he wasn't very impressive, going 9-13 with St. Louis. But the next season, he was traded to Chicago, and he soon helped turn the Cubbies into one of the best teams in baseball history. In 1906, they won 116 games, a record that stood alone until it was tied by the Seattle Mariners in 2001. From 1906 to 1910, they played in four World Series, winning two of them.

They did it mostly with pitching and defense. A newspaper columnist in Chicago even wrote a little piece of doggerel about their double-play combination of Joe Tinker, Johnny Evers, and Frank Chance, which has become part of baseball lore. It went, in part:

These are the saddest of possible words:
"Tinker to Evers to Chance."
Trio of bear cubs, and fleeter than birds,
Tinker and Evers and Chance.

They were good, but the team's best player by far was Brown. This is how good he was: From 1906 through 1909, his winning percentage averaged .773 and was never below .750. If a way to measure greatness is simply measuring wins against losses, there is no pitcher in major league history who had a better streak than Brown. In Walter Johnson's best four consecutive years, from 1912 through 1915, he had a .713 winning percentage. In Mathewson's best four years, from 1907 to 1910, his winning percentage was .748. The modern pitcher with the best winning percentage is Greg Maddux. His best four consecutive years in terms of winning percentage were from 1994 to 1997, when his winning percentage was .750. Here's another difference between them. Brown won 102 games during his best four years; Maddux won 75.

But Brown wasn't great only for four years. His lifetime winning percentage of .649 is 15th all-time (a standing that will improve as active players now ahead of him age and pitch less effectively). Even more impressive is his lifetime ERA: 2.06. That's third all-time. His 1.04 ERA in 1906 is the second lowest ERA ever recorded. Only Dutch Leonard's 1.01 in 1914 was better.

Here's another measure of greatness: How good are you against the best? In the first decade of the 20th century, Brown and Christy Mathewson were generally regarded as the league's top hurlers. Their head-to-head matchups had all the tension of a heavyweight championship boxing match. In Brown's rookie year, 1903, the two faced each other for the first time on June 13. In one of the most remarkable games ever, both men had no-hitters going into the ninth inning. Brown lost the no-hitter—and the game—in the ninth. But that was the last time Matty would beat Brown until 1909, after Three Finger had reeled off nine straight victories over his archrival.

It wasn't just Mathewson and Brown who were rivals; the Cubs and Matty's Giants were real enemies. In 1908, they were part of a pennant race that many people believe was the most exciting in baseball history. Chicago, New York, and Pittsburgh fought tooth and nail for the National League flag from opening day to the end of the season. When it was all over, the Giants and the Cubs were tied. A one-game play-off was needed to decide it all.

These were rough-and-tumble times. Before the game, the Cubs got word that the Giants' manager, John McGraw, intended to have two of his players start a fight with the Cubs during batting practice in the hope that the fans would riot. McGraw figured that since they were playing in the Giants' Polo Grounds, the umps would be fearful of the crowds' reaction and declare the Giants the winners on a forfeit. McGraw did send his players to instigate an argument, but the Cubs wouldn't take the bait.

Even so, it was a frightening situation. The stands were sold out. Giants' fans sat on the field in front of the bleachers. They even sat on the subway tracks that overlooked the field, preventing the trains from operating. A mob outside the park set fire to the left-field fence. When they broke through and got inside the stadium, mounted police had to drive them back.

The hated Cubs took most of the abuse, though. "I never heard anybody or any set of men called as many foul names as the Giants fans called us that day from the time we showed up till it was over," Brown recalled years later.

Since Brown had started or relieved in 11 of the team's last 14 games, the Cubs' player-manager, Frank Chance, decided to start Jack Pfiester against Mathewson and keep Brown ready, just in case. When Pfiester gave up a run in the first inning, Chance didn't hesitate to bring in his ace. There were two on and two out with the Cubs behind, 1-0, when Brown took the ball from his manager. By the ninth, the score was 4-2, Chicago. Brown held the Giants to four hits and a run for the win and the pennant. When the game ended, the Cubs ran for their lives. Three of them were beaten by the mob. Pfiester was stabbed with a knife. The Cubs had to barricade themselves inside the clubhouse and were able to leave the stadium only after a cordon of police brandishing revolvers escorted them out.

Brown not only pitched the game of his life, he nearly pitched the last game of his life.

More numbers

Brown's 56 shutouts are eighth all-time. Brown earned a 5-4 record in four World Series. Three of his five wins were shutouts. He never pitched a no-hitter, but he did pitch seven one-hitters. He was also a terrific reliever, who led the league in saves four times (a statistic that was compiled many years later). Here's one more interesting number about Brown: 1876, the year he was born, was the same year as America's centennial. To celebrate, his parents added the extra middle name, making him the only Hall of Famer named for a holiday.

Throwing Strikes

At his peak, his winning percentages were among the best ever, and winning is the name of the game. His ERA is the third lowest all-time. He consistently defeated his biggest rival, Christy Mathewson.

Throwing Balls

He never led the league in winning percentage and despite playing for a great team, he led the league in wins only once and in ERA only once.

Steven Norman Carlton (Lefty)

b. December 22, 1944, Miami, Florida
Career: 1965–1988
Record: 329-244
Guess which hand he threw with?

When Steve Carlton won 27 games for the Philadelphia Phillies in 1972, people said it had to be one of the best years ever by a pitcher. "Twenty-seven games? What's the big deal?" I bet you're saying. "Plenty of pitchers have won more than that in a season."

That's true. But consider this: Carlton was pitching for the worst team in the league. The rest of the pitching staff combined for only 32 victories. The team's batting star was Greg Luzinski, who had 18 home runs and a .281 average. Carlton had to do it all himself, and he did, leading the league in wins, earned run average, complete games, innings, and strikeouts. He was also second in shutouts. At one point, he won 15 games in a row and he allowed only one earned run in 63 innings. Imagine what his record would have been if he had been playing for even a mediocre team.

Carlton wasn't an easy guy to like. In spring training during his rookie season, he was pitching to Tim McCarver, who was one of the finest receivers in the league. After the game, Carlton rushed up to McCarver and told him, "Hey, you've got to call more breaking pitches when we're behind in the count."

McCarver couldn't believe he was hearing this from a rookie. He pushed Carlton up against the wall and let him have it. "You S.O.B!" McCarver yelled at him. "You've got a lot of guts telling me that. What credentials do you have?"

The next day McCarver apologized. But Carlton didn't, which was already typical of the young pitcher. He was such a headache that when he got into a salary dispute with the team's management that came down to a difference of $10,000, the Cardinals' general manager decided Carlton wasn't worth the trouble and traded him to the Phillies for Rick Wise, a decent pitcher who otherwise would never be mentioned in this book. Needless to say, it was one of the worst trades ever made. Carlton went on to have five 20-win seasons and capture four Cy Young Awards for Philadelphia.

That doesn't mean he wasn't a pain in the you-know-what for the Phillies. But he more than made up for it by becoming one of the best pitchers in the game. One thing the Phillies did do was bring in McCarver to be Lefty's personal catcher. More than anyone, McCarver understood that Carlton's single-minded attitude was the key to his greatness. In turn, Carlton trusted McCarver, and the two formed a formidable partnership in Philadelphia. "When Steve and I die, we are going to be buried in the same cemetery, sixty feet six inches apart," McCarver would joke.

Carlton obviously had great natural ability, but much of his success came because he worked harder than everyone else. When he arrived in the big leagues, scouts doubted that he could get his fastball by the hitters, so Carlton created a workout routine for himself that not only made him stronger but also turned him into the best-conditioned player in the game. Some of his exercise routines were incredible. To increase his stamina, he would run in place in a big vat of rice, where every step seemed like running a mile.

In 1969, he developed a deadly slider to go along with his fastball. Coming out of his three-quarter delivery, the ball would look like a fastball. But at the last second, it would explode downward and in on right-handed hitters, and they were helpless against it.

"Hitting against Carlton is like drinking coffee with a fork," said Hall of Fame slugger Willie Stargell.

Carlton's numbers back that up. He won 329 games, second among left-handers to Warren Spahn and 29 more than Lefty Grove. He also left southpaws Carl Hubbell and Sandy Koufax in the dust when it came to wins. Four times he led the league in wins. He was first in strikeouts five times, and his 4,136 lifetime strikeouts are second only to Nolan Ryan.

For a guy who was once told he wasn't strong enough, Carlton turned into a real workhorse. He lasted 24 years in the majors, leading the league in games started four times and in complete games three times.

Maybe the most significant measure of achievement is his four Cy Young Awards. The award is given annually to the best pitcher in each league. Carlton was the first to win it four times. Spahn won it once (although, to his credit, Spahnie won it when it was given to the best pitcher in both leagues); Ryan never did.

The only people Carlton hated more than hitters were reporters. For 15 years, he refused to talk to the press. Nobody ever knew why. Only in his last year, when he was trying to hang on with several clubs, did he loosen up. It prompted writers to repeat an old line used about another ballplayer: "He learned to say hello when it was time to say good-bye." After Carlton retired, he gave a long interview that revealed he was very prejudiced, so maybe it was better for everyone that he had refused to be interviewed all those years.

More numbers

He made the all-star team 10 times. He had a 2.56 ERA in four World Series. Carlton's 5,217 innings are ninth all-time. He was the unanimous choice for both the Cy Young and Most Valuable Player Awards in 1972, even though he pitched for a last-place team.

Throwing Strikes

His 1972 season was one of the best ever by any pitcher. He was a strikeout pitcher who was also a great winner and one of the most intense competitors ever to take the mound.

Throwing Balls

He was the ERA champ only once. He surrendered the most hits in the league four times.

John Gibson Clarkson

b. July 1, 1861, Cambridge, Massachusetts
d. February 4, 1909, Belmont, Massachusetts
Career: 1882, 1884–1894
Record: 326-177
Right-handed

John Clarkson had the talent to make him one of the top pitchers of the 19th century, but with his high-strung personality it didn't come easy. In the end, it probably cost him his life.

When Clarkson died in a mental hospital at the age of 47, his old manager, Hall of Famer Adrian "Cap" Anson, fondly recalled his former workhorse, praising his abilities but also remembering how difficult it was to get the best out of him. "Clarkson was one of the greatest pitchers of all time, certainly the best Chicago ever had," said Anson. "But not many know of his peculiar temperament and the amount of encouragement needed to keep him going. Scold him, find fault with him, and he could not pitch at all. Praise him, and he was unbeatable."

Clarkson was a member of a local Boston team when he met George Wright, the founder of the Cincinnati Redlegs, the legendary National League team that went undefeated in 1869. It was Wright who taught Clarkson the finer points of the game. In 1884, Clarkson was a backup pitcher and utility fielder for Saginaw of the Northwestern League when he was asked to pitch a three-game series against a powerful Detroit team. Clarkson won all three games, surrendering only one run in the process. That was when he was discovered by Anson. And when Clarkson's team disbanded that summer, Anson signed him to a contract with Chicago.

Apparently, it didn't take long for Anson to figure out how to handle his sensitive star. In 1885, Clarkson's first full year in the league, he won 53 games for the pennant-winning White Sox, losing only 16. He led the league in shutouts with 10 and in strikeouts with 308. His 53 wins represented well over half of the team's 87 wins. Imagine: If Roger Clemens had won the same percentage of the Yankees' victories in 2001, he would have been a 58-game winner! Clarkson won more than 30 games five years in a row. In three of the five years, he led the league in complete games. Four times he was the leader in innings pitched and three times in strikeouts. His lifetime winning percentage of .648 was by far the highest of the period, with the exception of Larry Corcoran, who spent only five years in the league.

Clarkson arrived in the National League as a fastball pitcher but soon developed a bewildering assortment of curve balls and a change of pace that he threw with great control. He also had something else up his sleeve—or on his waist. He had a silver belt buckle that he polished and wore when he pitched. On the mound he would wriggle around so the buckle would reflect the sun's glare into the batter's eyes.

Like Andy Pettitte or Roger Clemens, Clarkson had a way of glowering at hitters from under his cap that would intimidate them before he even threw the ball with his slow, deliberate motion. Mostly, though, he was a thinking pitcher who kept a mental book on every hitter he faced.

"In knowing exactly what kind of ball a batter could not hit and in his ability to serve up just that kind of a ball, I don't think I have ever seen the equal of Clarkson," said Anson.

Even though he was one of the game's first intimidators, he was not above a little humor. In those days, ballparks didn't have any lights. Sometimes, it got dark before a game ended. Clarkson was pitching one such game. When he appealed to the umpire to call the match, the ump refused, saying there was plenty of light. Clarkson then grabbed a lemon from the bench and tossed it over the plate. The umpire called it a strike. When Clarkson's catcher held the "ball" in front of the ump's face, the contest was stopped immediately.

Clarkson pitched the White Sox to two pennants, but after winning 38 games for them in 1887, he was sold to Boston for what was then the shocking sum of $10,000. The deal was the most sensational baseball transaction of the 19th century. It turned out to be a good deal for Boston. Clarkson averaged 35 wins a season over the next four years. In 1889, he enjoyed one of the best years any pitcher has ever had. He led the league in wins with 49, as well as winning percentage, earned run average, games, complete games, shutouts, innings, and strikeouts. Despite his heroics, Boston finished second to the Giants when Clarkson was defeated by fifth-place Pittsburgh on the last day of the season.

Over his 12-year career, he averaged more than 27 wins a season, which is higher than his other 19th-century rivals: Pud Galvin (26), Charles Radbourn (26), Tim Keefe (25), and Mickey Welch (24).

He retired after the 1894 season to open a cigar shop. Ten years later, a small item in a newspaper reported that he had been committed to a mental institution. He died five years later. Accounts written at the time of his death described him as a mental and physical wreck. He was only 47.

More Numbers

Clarkson was the game's second 300-game winner. In 12 years, he won three strikeout titles, which was then a major league record. His career strikeout total of 1,978 was a major league record for 22 years. He won more than 30 games in six of his 12 years in the majors.

Throwing Strikes

He averaged more wins and was a better strikeout pitcher than his 19th-century rivals.

Throwing Balls

His lifetime ERA was higher than that of other pitchers.

William Roger Clemens
(Roger, Rocket)

b. August 4, 1962, Dayton, Ohio
Career: 1983–
Right-handed

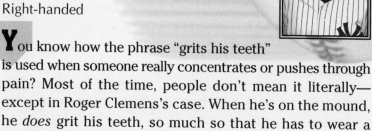

You know how the phrase "grits his teeth" is used when someone really concentrates or pushes through pain? Most of the time, people don't mean it literally— except in Roger Clemens's case. When he's on the mound, he *does* grit his teeth, so much so that he has to wear a mouth guard.

Now that's effort, but this is a guy who went 20-3 at the age of 39. You have to be a gritty guy to do that. Here's another example of how hard Clemens concentrates on the mound. On September 18, 1996, Clemens was working on a shutout against the Tigers. When the game was over and the Sox had won 4-0, his catcher, Bill Haselman, ran out to the mound to congratulate him.

"You know what you just did, right?" Haselman asked him.

"Yeah, I got the win and the shutout."

"You struck out twenty," Haselman said.

Clemens had no idea that he had just tied his own major league record for strikeouts in a game.

Clemens, who at age 40 still throws a fastball in the mid- to upper 90s, has always been physically and mentally tough. Most younger pitchers can't keep up with his heavy exercise regime. As for being mentally tough, all you have to do is look into his background to see where that came from.

Clemens's father and mother split up when he was less than a year old. His mother remarried, but his stepfather died suddenly when Roger was nine. His mother had to work three jobs to support her four children.

"I grew up extremely fast," Clemens said. "Watching my mother work the way she did . . . probably is what gave me my work ethic and drive and determination."

His high school coach later recalled having to tell Clemens to go home when it became too dark to practice. When he did go home, he watched films of pitchers and practiced throwing in front of a mirror.

"He learned that preparation is all-important," his coach said. "Nothing can happen unless you're prepared for it mentally and physically."

Of course, he was also born with a lot of natural ability. The curious thing about Clemens's talent, however, is that although he has earned a reputation as a hard thrower, in high school it wasn't his fastball that attracted the scouts. In fact, he was barely throwing in the 80s, and that scared away many scouts and colleges. He wasn't drafted; nor was he offered a scholarship by any major university.

But what he did have, even then, was phenomenal control. Finally, at San Jacinto Junior College, he broke 90 mph with his fastball. As a power pitcher who could also put the ball where he wanted, he attracted attention from the pros. But Roger decided to attend the University of Texas, which offered him a scholarship. Two years later, he signed with the Red Sox and he was on his way to a Hall of Fame career.

Clemens made his debut with Boston in 1984, but it wasn't until 1986 that he became the most feared pitcher in the league. That season, he led the league in wins and ERA while taking the Sox to the verge of a championship, failing only when Bill Buckner allowed an easy grounder to pass between his legs in Game 6 of the World Series.

On April 29, 1986, he broke the major league record for strikeouts in a nine-inning game when he set down 20 Seattle Mariners, surpassing the record previously held by Nolan Ryan, Steve Carlton, and Tom Seaver.

"I watched perfect games by Catfish Hunter and Mike Witt, but this was the most awesome pitching performance I've ever seen," said Red Sox manager John McNamara.

Clemens not only captured the Cy Young Award in 1986, he was also the league's MVP. He has since won five more Cy Young trophies, more than any other pitcher. He has also grabbed six ERA crowns. That's the most among active pitchers. His 293 wins are also first among active pitchers, as are his 3,909 career strikeouts, which place him third all-time behind Nolan Ryan and Steve Carlton.

"If Clemens is not the best, I'd hate to see who is," said pitcher Dan Plesac. "When they made the mold for pitchers, they made him. He's the perfect pitcher."

Clemens's success comes not only from his fastball and curve, but from a hard forkball that he calls Mr. Splitty. At six feet four inches and 235 pounds, and with a nasty temperament to boot, he is an intimidating figure on the mound. It doesn't hurt that he is also not afraid to come inside on a hitter, throwing a little "chin music," as it's called. It doesn't win him a lot of affection from opposing hitters (especially Mike Piazza, whom he beaned with an inside fastball in 2000), but it works when it comes to winning ball games. Old-timers would understand.

"Don Drysdale [who was famous for his brushback pitches] said something I've always enjoyed," Clemens once told a reporter. "He said, 'The most important pitch of the game is the second knockdown pitch.' Then the hitter knows the first one wasn't an accident. That's the way it is when I bust a guy twice."

More numbers.

He has led the league in wins four times, shutouts six times, and strikeouts five times. He was the first major leaguer to strike out 20 hitters in a nine-inning game, and the only pitcher to do it twice.

Throwing Strikes

An intimidator on the mound, with one of the hardest fastballs in major league history, Clemens is the complete package. Six Cy Young Awards indicate that, more often than not, he is the best of the best.

Throwing Balls

His postseason record has been mediocre. Even though he is a strikeout pitcher, he has never had a 300-strikeout season.

Jay Hanna Dean (Dizzy)

b. January 16, 1910, Lucas, Arkansas
d. July 17, 1974, Reno, Nevada
Career: 1930, 1932–1941, 1947
Record: 150-83
Right-handed

With the possible exception of Satchel Paige, no one ever took the mound with more confidence than Dizzy Dean. In the minors, he would tell his outfielders to sit down and rest while he did the work. Once he bet that he could strike out Vince DiMaggio four times in one game. He then struck him out three times—but in his fourth at-bat, DiMaggio popped the ball up behind the plate. As his catcher circled under the ball, Dean ran toward him, screaming, "Drop it, drop it!" because he wanted to win his bet. His catcher obliged, and Dean promptly fanned DiMaggio and collected his money.

Opposing players didn't always appreciate his strutting, but sportswriters loved Dean because he was so much fun. When one of them suggested that Dean was a braggart, the pitcher retorted, "It ain't braggin' if you can back it up."

And Diz could.

Jay Hanna Dean was pure country corn pone. His parents were poor Arkansas sharecroppers, so Jay and his brother, Paul, worked the fields all day and had little time for school. Neither boy got past fourth grade, but they didn't care. When they weren't working, they were doing what they loved most, running around the fields playing baseball—literally in the fields. When Dean pitched for his local team, cows grazed in right field. And the Deans were so poor, they often played barefoot.

In 1930, when Dean was signed by the Cardinals to his first minor league contract, he showed up with just the clothes on his back. "Where's your luggage?" his manager asked him. "I ain't got none," Dizzy answered.

Diz earned his nickname in the army. He had signed up when he was 16 because of the army's promise of three square meals a day and a workload that would be a lot easier than what he had on the farm. One day, he got bored peeling potatoes, so he entertained himself by throwing freshly peeled spuds at a garbage can. Suddenly, his sergeant appeared. "What are you doing," he yelled, "you dizzy S.O.B.?!"

But the sergeant also knew a pitcher when he saw one, and the teenager that everybody now called Dizzy was soon pitching baseballs instead of potatoes for the U.S. military. After a while, a Cardinal scout heard about him, and when his hitch was over, Dean signed with St. Louis for $300 a month.

He was brought up to the Cardinals in 1930 but got to pitch only one game—on the last day of the season. He threw a complete-game three-hitter, but when he goofed off in spring training the next season, he was sent back down. Finally, in 1932, he stuck with the club.

At six feet two inches tall and 180 pounds, Dizzy was long-limbed and surprisingly strong from his years toiling in the cotton fields. His pitching motion made perfect use of his size and strength. He employed a two-handed windup, reaching back as far as he could before whipping toward the plate. That gave his fastball blinding speed.

"Dean was a natural," said his manager. "He was the best fielding pitcher I ever saw. He could run the bases and when he was right, you didn't have to give him instructions, just the ball."

In his first full season, he led the league in innings pitched, strikeouts, and boasts. Before a game against the

Braves, he paid a visit to their dugout to let them in on his plans. "No curves today, fellas, just hard ones." He shut them out on three hits.

After fanning 17 Cubs in 1933 to set the National League mark for strikeouts in a game, he said, "Heck, if anybody told me I was settin' a record I'd of got me some more strikeouts."

He won 20 games in 1933. Then in 1934, he had the season that cemented his legend. He won 30 games and led the Gashouse Gang to the World Series championship. He was the first pitcher in 17 years to win 30, but that hardly tells the story of Dean's true brilliance that season.

Paul Dean had joined the Cardinals that year as a rookie. During spring training, the always confident Diz promised reporters, "Me 'n' Paul are gonna win 45 games this year."

For the first and last time, he underestimated himself. They won 49, which was more than half the games won by the entire team. The 1934 race between the Cardinals and the defending world champion New York Giants was one of the most exciting in history. The two teams were neck and neck the entire season. Over the last month, the two Dean boys pitched in two-thirds of the Cardinals' games, and with the Giants on their tail, every game was crucial. The pressure was unbelievable, but Dizzy and Paul were up to the task, and the Cardinals finally put the Giants away on the last weekend of the season.

By then, Dizzy had lost 20 pounds because of over-work, but he not only led the league with 30 wins, he also was second in ERA and saves and first in winning per-centage, strikeouts, shutouts, complete games, and in proclamations of his own huge talent. In the opener of a doubleheader on September 21, Dizzy pitched a complete-game three-hit shutout. Paul followed in the nightcap with a no-hitter. After the game, Dizzy said, "If I had known what Paul was gonna do, I would have pitched one, too."

Even sportswriters were overwhelmed by the Deans' performance in 1934.

"I've seen Matty pitch," wrote one scribe who had been covering baseball for nearly half a century, "and Walter Johnson and Cy Young, Rube Waddell, Addie Joss, Big Ed Walsh and Chief Bender, Grover Cleveland Alexander and Wee Willie Sherdel, and none of those great stars ever turned in such a feat as the Dean brothers have just completed."

But the Deans still had a World Series to play, and their opponents were the powerful Detroit Tigers, whose lineup included future Hall of Famers Mickey Cochrane, Charlie Gehringer, and Goose Goslin. They didn't scare Dizzy. Before the Series, he told reporters that he and Paul would win the Series all by themselves. It didn't quite work out that way, but they did win two games apiece, with Diz shutting out the Tigers in Game 7 to give St. Louis the crown.

The next year, Dizzy was nearly as good, winning 28 games and again leading the league in wins, complete games, innings pitched, and strikeouts. He had another excellent season in 1936, winning 24 games.

Then in 1937 disaster struck. He won 12 games in the first half of the season and was named to the all-star game. Dizzy begged off, saying he was tired, but the Cards' owner insisted he play. Dizzy was pitching in the third inning when Earl Averill smashed a line drive back to the mound that broke Dizzy's toe.

Although the toe was still sore, Dizzy was back on the mound 10 days later. The pain caused him to alter his delivery. Something snapped in his arm, and his fastball was gone. He was never the same again. In 1938, the Cardinals traded him to the Cubs. Relying on his curve, his change of pace, and his smarts, he still managed a 7-1 record in 13 games, with a 1.81 ERA, to help the Cubs win the pennant.

"His reputation was as a fastball pitcher, and he was plenty fast," said Hall of Famer Johnny Mize, "but he also knew how to pitch. He could throw you off with slow curves as well as anybody. He was a very deceptive fellow."

Still, Dizzy knew it was his last gasp. By 1940, he was pretty much through.

"There will never be another one like me," he told reporters before he retired. As usual, he was right.

More numbers

He led the league in strikeouts and complete games four straight years. He was also tops in innings pitched three times and in games twice. His lifetime winning percentage of .644 is 18th all-time.

Throwing Strikes

At his peak, he could put his money where his mouth was. It's hard to find a better year for a pitcher than the one Dizzy Dean had in 1934, leading the Cards to the championship and becoming the last National League pitcher to win 30 games.

Throwing Balls

While he had a terrific peak, it didn't last long—only four years. His 150 lifetime victories are far fewer than most of the greatest pitchers.

Robert William Andrew Feller
(Bob, Rapid Robert)

b. November 3, 1918, Van Meter, Iowa
Career: 1936–1941, 1945–1956
Record: 266-162
Right-handed

The first time a major league hitter faced a Bob Feller fastball, he ran and hid behind the water cooler.

It happened in 1936. Feller was 17 years old and had just signed with the Indians without having played a single day in the minors. Cleveland was playing an exhibition game against the Cardinals, whose famed Gashouse Gang lineup had some of the toughest veteran hitters in baseball.

Feller threw with a high kicking motion, which made his supersonic fastball almost impossible for the batter to follow. Even worse, Feller had little control over it. The first player up was Leo Durocher. Feller's first pitch went over Durocher's head. The next two went behind him. Finally, the teenager threw two strikes across the plate.

"You better watch yourself, Leo," the umpire taunted him. "The kid hasn't got the best control in the world."

Already stunned by Feller's speed, Durocher dashed into the Cardinal dugout.

"Get back out here and hit!" the umpire yelled at him. "You still have one strike left."

"You take it. I don't want it!" Durocher yelled back.

Finally, he did emerge, only to stand in the back of the batter's box and wave timidly at strike three. In three innings that day, Feller struck out eight Cardinals. After the game, photographers asked the great pitcher Dizzy Dean to pose with the youngster. Dean replied, "After what he did today, you'd better ask him if he'll pose with me."

The Cardinals weren't the only ones blown away by the teenager, who some said was faster than Walter Johnson. In his first actual start that August, Feller struck out 15 St. Louis Browns. Three weeks later, he fanned 17 Athletics, tying Dean's major league record for most strikeouts in a game.

Feller had signed with the Indians for one dollar and an autographed baseball. "And it wasn't even a new baseball," Feller wrote in his autobiography. After just half a season, he had already proved to be the best bargain in baseball history. But he would have signed for 50 cents. That's how badly he wanted to play big league baseball.

Growing up on a farm in Iowa, his father had wanted to play baseball, but he didn't have the opportunity, so he was determined that if young Robert wanted to play ball, he would. Even before he was 10 years old, Feller could throw a ball farther and harder than most teenagers. His father did all he could to help him. He built a batting cage from leftover lumber and chicken wire, and the two would practice pitching after their chores were done. In the winter, they played simulated games in the barn and talked baseball around the hot stove in the kitchen.

When Bob was 12, he and his father cut a baseball diamond out of one of their fields. It even had a grandstand and a scoreboard. Teams would come from out of town to play the local farm boys, but they didn't have much luck against Feller. As he grew to his full six feet, scouts began to take notice. He pitched seven games in high school. Five of them were no-hitters. Then he moved on to semipro ball. In his first start, he struck out 21 batters and pitched a no-hitter. He did give up a hit in his second start, but in that game he whiffed 23.

Feller pitched five no-hitters that season. Even the umpires were calling major league teams, begging them to send someone to see this kid, but no one seemed to believe the reports. Besides, the kid was only 16. Finally, a scout for the Indians decided that since he was checking out another pitcher in a nearby town, he might as well stop in Van Meter. He never made it to the other town. After seeing Feller pitch, he took young Bob and his Dad to a hotel room and signed Bob to an agreement on hotel stationery.

When Feller arrived in the majors months later, he overwhelmed hitters with his scattershot fastball. In one game, the Yankees' Hall of Fame pitcher Lefty Gomez, who was as funny as he was talented, came to the plate against Feller just as the sun was setting. As he entered the batter's box, he reached into his back pocket and took out a match. "C'mon, Lefty," the umpire said to him. "You know you can see Feller perfectly well." "Yeah," Gomez answered. "I just want to be sure he sees me."

Everyone immediately began comparing Feller to Johnson, but there was one huge difference between them: Feller had one of the best curve balls in the game. It would freeze hitters who were trying to time his heater. In fact, Feller always thought he struck out more batters with his curve than with his fastball. As if that weren't enough, he also had a terrific slider.

"He had more stuff than anybody," the great Ted Williams said of Feller.

He proved it on the last day of the 1938 season, when the Detroit Tigers came to Cleveland. Their first baseman, Hank Greenberg, had 58 home runs. Two more would tie Babe Ruth's major league record. When the game was over, he still had 58—and Feller had the new major league record for strikeouts in a game with 18.

"You couldn't hit the curve, so you'd wait for the fastball," said Greenberg, "but that would be by you before you knew what happened."

The next season was the first of Feller's three consecutive

20-win seasons. In each, he led the league in wins and strikeouts and innings pitched. In 1940, he pitched the first opening day no-hitter in major league history.

After the 1941 season, he had already notched his 107th win and 1,233rd strikeout and he wasn't even 23 years old! He was well on his way to 300 victories and topping Walter Johnson's lifetime record of 3,508 strikeouts. But on December 7, the Japanese bombed Pearl Harbor, and even though he could have gotten an exemption because his father was suffering from cancer, Feller enlisted in the navy. Now he was firing cannon shells instead of baseballs and he missed most of the next four seasons, earning battle stars instead of world championships.

He returned to the Indians at the end of the 1945 season. In 1946, he picked up right where he left off, leading the league in wins and shutouts. His 348 strikeouts were the most since Rube Waddell's 349 in 1904. He also tossed his second no-hitter and his eighth one-hitter, breaking Addie Joss's lifetime record.

Although he began to lose a few miles per hour on his fastball in the late 1940s, Feller felt that he became a better pitcher as he matured in his thinking on the mound. "In my early years I never learned to 'pitch,' because I didn't think I had to," Feller said. "I figured that even if I walked a few batters, I could power-pitch my way out of a jam. By the late forties things were different. I'd lost a lot of my steam and I realized I had to be a 'pitcher' out there, not just a thrower."

He made the adjustment successfully. He won 20 or more games twice more in his career and set a major league record with his third no-hitter. Had he not missed nearly four seasons in his prime, he probably would have won more than 350 games and easily passed Johnson for first on the all-time strikeout list. But Feller had no regrets.

To succeed, Ford said, "you need arm, heart, and
[hea]d. Arm and heart are assets. Head is a necessity."

Casey Stengel, "the Ol' Perfessor," said Ford was so
[sm]art, he was "my little perfessor." And he was so tough
[and] sure of himself for a little guy that Stengel also called
[him] "my banty rooster."

How confident was he? Many times on days that he
[pit]ched, he would set up a tablecloth in the bull pen and
[se]t down a bottle of wine with a candle in it. Ford said he
[figu]red that if the relievers weren't going to work that day
[th]ey might as well be comfortable.

Like an expert gambler, Whitey liked to play the per-
[ce]ntages. When he had an advantage on a hitter and the
[sit]uation called for a curve ball, Whitey would throw his
[fa]stball—because he knew it would surprise the batter.
[Ev]en if the hitter could get around on it, Ford knew the
[wi]de expanse of Yankee Stadium's outfield would swallow
[up] most long flies. "Whitey would pitch a guy right into
[hi]s power," said Yankee shortstop Tony Kubek. "In Yankee
[St]adium, he could get away with it."

In his book *61*, about the Yankees' brilliant 1961 season,
[K]ubek wrote that Ford knew exactly what he was doing
[w]ith almost every pitch.

"Whitey would stand behind the mound, rubbing up
[th]e ball. He might just catch my eye for a second and
[m]ove me with his eyes about ten feet toward second
[b]ase," Kubek wrote. "If he looked to his left, I moved left.
[T]o his right, I'd go right. Then a guy would hit a bullet
[ri]ght at me and couldn't believe I was playing in that spot.
[B]ut Whitey had set the whole thing up."

He won 236 games in his lifetime. He would have won
[m]any more except that he missed two full seasons to the
[m]ilitary during the Korean War. Stengel also liked to pitch
[F]ord on five days' rest and then save him for key games.

"Sure, I was disappointed," he said, "but I certainly
didn't feel sorry for myself. I came home from the war in
one piece. Many people didn't, so I'd say I was one of the
lucky ones."

More numbers

Feller finished his career with 12 one-hitters and six 20-
win seasons. He led the league in strikeouts seven times,
in innings pitched five times, in shutouts four times, and in
complete games three times. He appeared in only one World
Series and was a 1-0 loser in Game 1 against the Braves in
1948, because of a bad call by the umpire: In the ninth
inning, Feller clearly picked the Braves' Phil Masi off second
base, but the umpire called him safe. Masi then scored the
game's only run on a single.

Throwing Strikes

Feller's fastball was nearly as good as Johnson's, or better,
depending on whom you asked, but everyone agreed he
had more pitches than Johnson. His single-season high for
strikeouts topped Johnson's. Feller's marks for lifetime
no-hitters and one-hitters stood for years.

Throwing Balls

He led the league in walks four times and was tops in ERA
only once.

Edward Charles Ford (Whitey, The Chairman of the Board)

b. October 21, 1928, New York City
Career: 1950, 1953–1967
Record: 236-106
Left-handed

When people think of New Yorkers, they think of people who are sharp, brash, cocky, and tough. All those words perfectly describe Whitey Ford, a New York City kid who became as tough a pitcher as ever toed the mound.

People called Ford a "money pitcher," because in the big games, when money was on the line, he almost always came through. Even if he didn't have the most overwhelming stuff, he invariably figured out a way to win, and that's all any manager wants.

"Of all the left-handers I've ever seen, Whitey is the one I'd like to have going for me in the one must-win game," said Hall of Famer Enos Slaughter, who saw a lot of left-handers in his 19 major league seasons.

How good was Whitey in big games? Here are a few numbers: Ford's 10 World Series victories are the most in major league history. From 1960 to 1962, he threw 33⅔ consecutive scoreless innings over three World Series, breaking the record set by Babe Ruth in 1918. But he didn't excel just in the fall classic. Ford's lifetime .690 winning percentage is the best among all 20th-century pitchers who won 200 games or more.

When Ford was playing ball locally in Queens, New York, all three New York teams—the Giants, the Dodgers, and the Yankees—wanted to sign him, but he was a Yankee fan and he signed with them for a $7,000 bonus. Now, here's the kind of cocky kid he was: Once he got the money,

he cashed the check and headed to Times [...] his bankroll to the world. His outing end[...] wanted to know why a 16-year-old was car[...] that dough, and he sent him home for his o[...]

Ford played in the minors for three ye[...] Yankee manager Casey Stengel liked to tel[...] how that season he received an anonym[...] from someone who told him, "If you want to v[...] you'd better call up that kid Ford from Kan[...] always denied it, but Stengel went to his [...] was Whitey on the other end of the line.

Ford did help the Yankees capture the penn[...] nine straight games for the Bombers that su[...] won Game 4 of the World Series against the [...] gave New York its second of five consecutive c[...]

Ford was known for his great sense of fu[...] but he was all business on the mound. He p[...] smooth, economical windup that left him in pe[...] to field the ball. He also had a terrific pick-[...] could throw a fastball, curve, sinker, and sli[...] one of a number of different arm positions. H[...] other pitches that weren't exactly legal and [...] the ball do everything but the mambo. One [...] ball, which he would throw after rubbing dir[...] while picking up the rosin bag. The other was a[...] would throw that after using a ring on his fin[...] the ball. When the umpires caught on to [...] pitches, Ford enlisted his catcher, Elston How[...] out, so when the situation called for it, How[...] slyly rub the ball in the dirt or scrape it against a[...] edge of his shin guard before tossing it back to t[...]

To Ford, who was 5 feet 10 inches tall and 18[...] was all part of the process of outthinking hitter[...] n't outmuscle.

As a result, he didn't have his first 20-win season until 1961, when the Yankees' new manager, Ralph Houk, decided to pitch Ford on the standard four days' rest. He promptly went 25-4, leading the league not only in wins and winning percentage but also in games started and innings pitched. That quieted any whispers that he wasn't strong enough to withstand the rigors of a full season of starts. Two years later, at the age of 34, he won 24 and lost only 7, again leading the league in wins, winning percentage, games started, and innings pitched.

But, you say, he pitched for the Yankees. Even a monkey could have had a great winning percentage if it had pitched for the Yankees. True, but Ford's winning percentage was almost always higher than the team's, and this was a team that won 11 pennants and six championships while he was with them. Whitey was their ace of aces. That's why he was called "The Chairman of the Board."

More numbers

Until he hurt his arm in 1966, Ford never had a losing season. In 11 of his 16 seasons, his ERA was under 3.00. He had a lifetime 2.75 ERA, leading the league twice in that department. He was also tops three times in wins and winning percentage. He led the league in shutouts twice. Ford was a seven-time all-star. Besides wins and consecutive scoreless innings, he also holds World Series records for games started, innings, and strikeouts. He is second in shutouts and fourth in complete games.

Throwing Strikes

A bulldog and the very definition of a "money pitcher," Ford was the best left-hander on what many people think was the No. 1 team of all time. His .690 lifetime winning percentage says it all. If the best pitchers win the highest percentage of games, Whitey is your man.

Throwing Balls

He lost eight World Series games, also a record. Outside of winning percentage, his career numbers aren't as overwhelming as those of other pitchers.

James Francis Galvin (Pud)

b. December 25, 1856, St. Louis, Missouri
d. March 7, 1902, Pittsburgh, Pennsylvania
Career: 1875, 1879–1892
Record: 361-308
Right-handed

James Galvin's nickname was "Pud," because it was said that he turned opposing hitters into pudding. That might have been an exaggeration, but Galvin was baseball's first 300-game winner, and he won all those games over only 15 seasons and without ever playing on a championship team.

He was also the game's first great pick-off artist. In fact, though there are no numbers to support this, he may have had the best pick-off move ever. The classic story about Galvin is about a game in which he walked the first three hitters, loading the bases. He then proceeded to pick off each of them to get out of the inning unscathed. That's a record that will never be broken.

Galvin grew up in an Irish section of St. Louis known as "Kerry Patch." He was strong and stocky, and he trained to be a steam fitter (a person who repairs steampipes) until he realized he could throw a baseball faster than anybody had ever seen. In 1878, he joined the Buffalo Bisons, possibly the best minor league team ever assembled. With Galvin as their ace, the Bisons played 17 games against major league teams and won 10 of them. The next season they were admitted into the National League, and they finished third.

Although Galvin pitched in the underhand style of the day, he not only had blazing speed, but he could put the ball where he wanted it, whether throwing to the first base-man or the catcher.

"If I had Galvin to catch, no one would ever steal a base on me," said the Giants' Hall of Fame catcher Buck Ewing. "That fellow keeps 'em glued to the base, and he also has the best control of any pitcher in the league."

How good was his control? Over his 14 years in the majors, he averaged 1.1 walks a game. Among other Hall of Fame hurlers of the 19th century, Hoss Radbourn averaged 1.7 and John Clarkson 2.4. Galvin won more than 20 games 10 times. In 1883, he won 46 games and led the league in games and innings pitched, but 1884, the year Radbourn won 60 games, was also probably Galvin's best year. He started 72 games and completed 71 of them, winning 46 with 22 losses, for a .676 winning percentage. His 12 shutouts led the league for the second year in a row. Galvin was simply amazing at times. From August 2 to August 8, the Bisons played a series at Detroit. On August 2, he pitched a one-hitter. Two days later, he pitched a no-hitter. Three days later, he pitched another shutout and then the next day, he finally lost, 1-0, in 12 innings. That's one run in 39 innings. He also struck out 36 without walking a single batter. Later that season, when Radbourn won 18 straight for Providence, it was Galvin who stopped his streak by outdueling Old Hoss.

More Numbers

Galvin was a workhorse his entire career. His 5,941 lifetime innings are second all-time behind Cy Young, who played eight more years than Galvin. Galvin is also second lifetime in games completed and eleventh in career shutouts with 57. His 361 wins are sixth all-time. His 639 complete games are a National League record.

"Sure, I was disappointed," he said, "but I certainly didn't feel sorry for myself. I came home from the war in one piece. Many people didn't, so I'd say I was one of the lucky ones."

More numbers

Feller finished his career with 12 one-hitters and six 20-win seasons. He led the league in strikeouts seven times, in innings pitched five times, in shutouts four times, and in complete games three times. He appeared in only one World Series and was a 1-0 loser in Game 1 against the Braves in 1948, because of a bad call by the umpire: In the ninth inning, Feller clearly picked the Braves' Phil Masi off second base, but the umpire called him safe. Masi then scored the game's only run on a single.

Throwing Strikes

Feller's fastball was nearly as good as Johnson's, or better, depending on whom you asked, but everyone agreed he had more pitches than Johnson. His single-season high for strikeouts topped Johnson's. Feller's marks for lifetime no-hitters and one-hitters stood for years.

Throwing Balls

He led the league in walks four times and was tops in ERA only once.

Edward Charles Ford (Whitey, The Chairman of the Board)

b. October 21, 1928, New York City
Career: 1950, 1953–1967
Record: 236-106
Left-handed

When people think of New Yorkers, they think of people who are sharp, brash, cocky, and tough. All those words perfectly describe Whitey Ford, a New York City kid who became as tough a pitcher as ever toed the mound.

People called Ford a "money pitcher," because in the big games, when money was on the line, he almost always came through. Even if he didn't have the most overwhelming stuff, he invariably figured out a way to win, and that's all any manager wants.

"Of all the left-handers I've ever seen, Whitey is the one I'd like to have going for me in the one must-win game," said Hall of Famer Enos Slaughter, who saw a lot of left-handers in his 19 major league seasons.

How good was Whitey in big games? Here are a few numbers: Ford's 10 World Series victories are the most in major league history. From 1960 to 1962, he threw 33⅔ consecutive scoreless innings over three World Series, breaking the record set by Babe Ruth in 1918. But he didn't excel just in the fall classic. Ford's lifetime .690 winning percentage is the best among all 20th-century pitchers who won 200 games or more.

When Ford was playing ball locally in Queens, New York, all three New York teams—the Giants, the Dodgers, and the Yankees—wanted to sign him, but he was a Yankee fan and he signed with them for a $7,000 bonus. Now, here's the kind of cocky kid he was: Once he got the money, he cashed the check and headed to Times Square to flash his bankroll to the world. His outing ended when a cop wanted to know why a 16-year-old was carrying around all that dough, and he sent him home for his own safety.

Ford played in the minors for three years, until 1950. Yankee manager Casey Stengel liked to tell a story about how that season he received an anonymous phone call from someone who told him, "If you want to win the pennant, you'd better call up that kid Ford from Kansas City." Ford always denied it, but Stengel went to his grave saying it was Whitey on the other end of the line.

Ford did help the Yankees capture the pennant by winning nine straight games for the Bombers that summer. He then won Game 4 of the World Series against the Phillies, which gave New York its second of five consecutive championships.

Ford was known for his great sense of fun off the field, but he was all business on the mound. He pitched with a smooth, economical windup that left him in perfect position to field the ball. He also had a terrific pick-off move. He could throw a fastball, curve, sinker, and slider from any one of a number of different arm positions. He also threw other pitches that weren't exactly legal and which made the ball do everything but the mambo. One was a mud-ball, which he would throw after rubbing dirt on the ball while picking up the rosin bag. The other was a cut ball. He would throw that after using a ring on his finger to scuff the ball. When the umpires caught on to both those pitches, Ford enlisted his catcher, Elston Howard, to help out, so when the situation called for it, Howard would slyly rub the ball in the dirt or scrape it against a sharpened edge of his shin guard before tossing it back to the mound.

To Ford, who was 5 feet 10 inches tall and 180 pounds, it was all part of the process of outthinking hitters he couldn't outmuscle.

To succeed, Ford said, "you need arm, heart, and head. Arm and heart are assets. Head is a necessity."

Casey Stengel, "the Ol' Perfessor," said Ford was so smart, he was "my little perfessor." And he was so tough and sure of himself for a little guy that Stengel also called him "my banty rooster."

How confident was he? Many times on days that he pitched, he would set up a tablecloth in the bull pen and put down a bottle of wine with a candle in it. Ford said he figured that if the relievers weren't going to work that day they might as well be comfortable.

Like an expert gambler, Whitey liked to play the percentages. When he had an advantage on a hitter and the situation called for a curve ball, Whitey would throw his fastball—because he knew it would surprise the batter. Even if the hitter could get around on it, Ford knew the wide expanse of Yankee Stadium's outfield would swallow up most long flies. "Whitey would pitch a guy right into his power," said Yankee shortstop Tony Kubek. "In Yankee Stadium, he could get away with it."

In his book *61*, about the Yankees' brilliant 1961 season, Kubek wrote that Ford knew exactly what he was doing with almost every pitch.

"Whitey would stand behind the mound, rubbing up the ball. He might just catch my eye for a second and move me with his eyes about ten feet toward second base," Kubek wrote. "If he looked to his left, I moved left. To his right, I'd go right. Then a guy would hit a bullet right at me and couldn't believe I was playing in that spot. But Whitey had set the whole thing up."

He won 236 games in his lifetime. He would have won many more except that he missed two full seasons to the military during the Korean War. Stengel also liked to pitch Ford on five days' rest and then save him for key games.

As a result, he didn't have his first 20-win season until 1961, when the Yankees' new manager, Ralph Houk, decided to pitch Ford on the standard four days' rest. He promptly went 25-4, leading the league not only in wins and winning percentage but also in games started and innings pitched. That quieted any whispers that he wasn't strong enough to withstand the rigors of a full season of starts. Two years later, at the age of 34, he won 24 and lost only 7, again leading the league in wins, winning percentage, games started, and innings pitched.

But, you say, he pitched for the Yankees. Even a monkey could have had a great winning percentage if it had pitched for the Yankees. True, but Ford's winning percentage was almost always higher than the team's, and this was a team that won 11 pennants and six championships while he was with them. Whitey was their ace of aces. That's why he was called "The Chairman of the Board."

More numbers

Until he hurt his arm in 1966, Ford never had a losing season. In 11 of his 16 seasons, his ERA was under 3.00. He had a lifetime 2.75 ERA, leading the league twice in that department. He was also tops three times in wins and winning percentage. He led the league in shutouts twice. Ford was a seven-time all-star. Besides wins and consecutive scoreless innings, he also holds World Series records for games started, innings, and strikeouts. He is second in shutouts and fourth in complete games.

Throwing Strikes

A bulldog and the very definition of a "money pitcher," Ford was the best left-hander on what many people think was the No. 1 team of all time. His .690 lifetime winning percentage says it all. If the best pitchers win the highest percentage of games, Whitey is your man.

Throwing Balls

He lost eight World Series games, also a record. Outside of winning percentage, his career numbers aren't as overwhelming as those of other pitchers.

James Francis Galvin (Pud)

b. December 25, 1856, St. Louis, Missouri
d. March 7, 1902, Pittsburgh, Pennsylvania
Career: 1875, 1879–1892
Record: 361-308
Right-handed

James Galvin's nickname was "Pud," because it was said that he turned opposing hitters into pudding. That might have been an exaggeration, but Galvin was baseball's first 300-game winner, and he won all those games over only 15 seasons and without ever playing on a championship team.

He was also the game's first great pick-off artist. In fact, though there are no numbers to support this, he may have had the best pick-off move ever. The classic story about Galvin is about a game in which he walked the first three hitters, loading the bases. He then proceeded to pick off each of them to get out of the inning unscathed. That's a record that will never be broken.

Galvin grew up in an Irish section of St. Louis known as "Kerry Patch." He was strong and stocky, and he trained to be a steam fitter (a person who repairs steampipes) until he realized he could throw a baseball faster than anybody had ever seen. In 1878, he joined the Buffalo Bisons, possibly the best minor league team ever assembled. With Galvin as their ace, the Bisons played 17 games against major league teams and won 10 of them. The next season they were admitted into the National League, and they finished third.

Although Galvin pitched in the underhand style of the day, he not only had blazing speed, but he could put the ball where he wanted it, whether throwing to the first baseman or the catcher.

"If I had Galvin to catch, no one would ever steal a base on me," said the Giants' Hall of Fame catcher Buck Ewing. "That fellow keeps 'em glued to the base, and he also has the best control of any pitcher in the league."

How good was his control? Over his 14 years in the majors, he averaged 1.1 walks a game. Among other Hall of Fame hurlers of the 19th century, Hoss Radbourn averaged 1.7 and John Clarkson 2.4. Galvin won more than 20 games 10 times. In 1883, he won 46 games and led the league in games and innings pitched, but 1884, the year Radbourn won 60 games, was also probably Galvin's best year. He started 72 games and completed 71 of them, winning 46 with 22 losses, for a .676 winning percentage. His 12 shutouts led the league for the second year in a row. Galvin was simply amazing at times. From August 2 to August 8, the Bisons played a series at Detroit. On August 2, he pitched a one-hitter. Two days later, he pitched a no-hitter. Three days later, he pitched another shutout and then the next day, he finally lost, 1-0, in 12 innings. That's one run in 39 innings. He also struck out 36 without walking a single batter. Later that season, when Radbourn won 18 straight for Providence, it was Galvin who stopped his streak by outdueling Old Hoss.

More Numbers

Galvin was a workhorse his entire career. His 5,941 lifetime innings are second all-time behind Cy Young, who played eight more years than Galvin. Galvin is also second lifetime in games completed and eleventh in career shutouts with 57. His 361 wins are sixth all-time. His 639 complete games are a National League record.

Throwing Strikes

He was baseball's first 300-game winner and maybe the greatest control pitcher of the 19th century. His record doesn't indicate that he played mostly for mediocre teams.

Throwing Balls

His 308 losses are second highest all-time.

Robert Gibson (Bob)

b. November 9, 1935, Omaha, Nebraska
Career: 1959–1975
Record: 251-174
Right-handed

Bob Gibson was one intense dude. Here's an example: In the ninth inning of Game 1 of the 1968 World Series, he had just fanned Al Kaline for his 15th strikeout of the game, tying a World Series record. (He would finish with 17.) The home crowd went wild. His catcher, Tim McCarver, gestured to Gibson to turn around and look at the scoreboard so he could appreciate for himself what all the fuss was about. Gibson refused. McCarver gestured again. Again, Gibson shook his head. He had no idea what they were screaming about and he didn't care. "Throw the damned ball back, will you?" he shouted to McCarver. "C'mon, c'mon, c'mon, let's go!"

That was Gibson. Though he was engaging and fun in the clubhouse, on the mound he had no friends, even among his teammates. The mound was his office, and he had a No Trespassing sign permanently hanging on the door.

"If batters who made outs ran across the mound on their way back to their dugouts, he'd stare them down and hit them the next time up," recalled McCarver. "You didn't get on his turf. When I'd go out to the mound, he'd say angrily, 'All you know about pitching is that it's hard to hit.'"

"He was the most intimidating player in the league," said Ted Simmons, who caught for Gibson for several years. "He'd stare in at the batter, and I could feel his eyes burn. He went to war against every hitter he faced. He never gave in and never gave up. He won by force of his personality, and by his concentration."

All-star games are a treat for most players. Taking a mid-season break, they generally enjoy setting aside their rivalries for a couple of days and appreciating the camaraderie of fellow pros. Not Gibson. He played in seven all-star games and made friends in none of them. "These guys, two days later, they're going to try to beat my brains out," he explained after he retired. "And I always felt—and I still feel today—that when people don't know anything about you they have a tendency to fear you."

Even at home, he couldn't stand to lose. "I've played a couple hundred games of tic-tac-toe with my little daughter, and she hasn't beaten me yet," he said matter-of-factly. "I've always had to win. I've got to win."

That's why he did win. Something inside him said he had no choice. Gibson needed that inner force just to make it through childhood. He was a sickly infant. Growing up, he suffered from rickets and asthma and nearly died. His father died before he was born. His mother worked at a menial job to support her seven children.

As a teenager, Bob found an outlet in sports, although he had to get permission to participate in school athletics after a physical examination revealed he had a heart murmur. He went to Creighton University, where he became a star basketball player. He was such a great jumper that he could touch the basket with his elbow. While he was in school, he even played for the Harlem Globetrotters basketball team. Baseball was secondary to Gibson, but the Cardinals saw him pitching in 1957, and they offered him a contract for $3,000 and a $1,000 signing bonus. He accepted it and began his pro career in the minors.

Many athletes like Gibson who came of age in the 1960s were inspired by the civil rights movement.

Understandably, many reacted in rage to the racism that infected much of American society. Having experienced segregation, Gibson felt that anger and channeled it along with his competitiveness and ability into a Hall of Fame career.

Gibson always seemed to be pitching in a rage. He launched his overpowering fastball with the force of his entire body, not just his arm. In 1961, he improved on it when he discovered by accident that by altering the way he gripped the baseball he could make it dart in different directions.

It took a few years for Gibson to harness the control on his fastball, but once he did he became one of the most dominating pitchers of the 1960s and 1970s. In 1962, he led the league with five shutouts. In 1965, he enjoyed the first of five 20-win seasons.

Gibson's 1968 season has to rank with the best of all time. His earned run average was an astonishing 1.12, breaking Grover Cleveland Alexander's National League mark of 1.22 for a pitcher with 300 or more innings in a season. Alexander's mark was set in 1915. Of Gibson's 22 wins, 13 were shutouts. He also led the league with 268 strikeouts. Of the 34 games he started, he completed 28 of them. At one point in the season, he won 15 games in a row and during one stretch he gave up only two runs in 92 innings. Maybe the most amazing thing about that season was how he ever lost nine games. You can blame the Cardinal hitters for that. In those nine outings, he gave up a total of 27 runs.

McCarver looked at it in his own humorous way. "Bob Gibson is the luckiest pitcher I ever saw," he said. "He always pitches when the other team doesn't score any runs."

In World Series competition, Gibson was spectacular. The race for the National League pennant in 1964 came

right down to the wire. Gibson pitched twice during the last weekend to help nail down the flag for the Cardinals. He then pitched three times in the World Series, losing Game 2 but returning to win Game 5. Then, on two days' rest against a brutal Yankee lineup, Gibson was called on by his manager, Johnny Keane, to try to close out the Series with a win for the Cards. Right from the start, Gibson was visibly tired. He had to take deep breaths before every pitch, but he managed to hang on for a 7-5 win. Asked afterward why he decided to go with his obviously exhausted star, Keane said, "I had a commitment to his heart."

Three years later, Gibson and the Cardinals faced the Boston Red Sox in the fall classic. Gibson limited the Sox to six hits for a 2-1 complete-game victory in Game 1. He improved on that in Game 4 with a five-hit shutout and then capped it off with a three-hitter in Game 7. He completed all three games, allowing only 14 hits and 3 runs in 27 innings.

The next year, he picked up right where he'd left off. After striking out 17 Tigers in Game 1 of the World Series, he pitched another complete-game victory in Game 4. It was also his second win in a head-to-head match-up against Detroit's 31-game winner, Denny McLain. In Game 7, Gibson was even stronger, but he was unable to cap his brilliant season with a second consecutive World Series ring, as a crucial misplay in the field let him down. The Cardinals lost, 4-1, even though Gibson surrendered only eight hits in nine innings.

He never played in another World Series, much to the relief of the American League. His seven World Series wins are second only to Whitey Ford's, although Ford pitched in 11 World Series, as compared with Gibson's three. His 92 strikeouts are second to Ford's 94. But again, that number is deceiving. Ford got his 94 in 146 innings;

Gibson did it in 81. Gibson's 10.2 strikeouts per nine innings lead all pitchers.

More numbers

Gibson was the National League's Most Valuable Player in 1968 and the MVP of two World Series, in 1964 and 1967. He won the Cy Young Award in 1968 and 1970. A terrific fielder, he won the Gold Glove Award for pitchers every year from 1965 to 1973. He struck out over 200 batters a season nine times. He retired as the second pitcher in major league history to record over 3,000 strikeouts.

He was a leader in shutouts four times.

Throwing Strikes

A frightening intimidator on the mound, Gibson was even better in the clutch, as he showed in his seven World Series victories. His 1968 season was simply incredible.

Throwing Balls

He didn't lead the league in as many categories as other pitchers. Many other pitchers also had terrific seasons in 1968.

Robert Moses Grove (Lefty)

b. March 6, 1900, Lonaconing, Maryland
d. May 22, 1975, Norwalk, Ohio
Career: 1925–1941
Record: 300-141
Left-handed (It would be pretty weird if he weren't.)

Lefty Grove was so fast, someone said he could throw a lamb chop past a wolf. Indeed, probably the only thing more fiery than Grove's fastball was his temper.

When Grove was upset, he didn't just sulk or scream. He broke things, he kicked things, he threw things—even things that were nailed down. During 1931, Grove's best year, he won 16 games in a row. On August 23, he was going for No. 17 against the St. Louis Browns. A win would have given him the American League record. That day, the A's Hall of Fame left fielder Al Simmons had to leave town to see his doctor. His replacement blew an easy fly ball. The Athletics lost, 1-0, and Grove's streak was over.

Grove stormed into the locker room, cursing Simmons. In a matter of seconds, the place looked as if it had been hit by a tornado.

"I tore those steel lockers off the wall, ripped my uniform up, threw everything I could get my hands on—bats, balls, shoes, gloves, and benches," Grove recalled many years after he retired. "He should have been there. I won six or seven in a row after that. I would have won twenty-four straight games. It still gets me mad when I think about it."

Nearly every teammate had a story about his temper, but they also were in awe of his fastball, which was said to be right up there with Walter Johnson's. One time a company that made plate glass said it had perfected a pane that was shatterproof. To test it, they set it up over home plate and challenged Grove to break it with a pitch. Grove wound up and threw a fastball right through it.

"Sometimes, when the sun was out really bright, he would throw that baseball in there, and it looked like a flash of white sewing thread coming at you," said Joe Sewell, who hit against Grove many times.

Grove's fastball was so good that he hardly threw anything else—until a sore arm caused him to develop a second pitch after 1934. That meant the hitters knew exactly what was coming, but they still couldn't do anything about it. "Inning after inning, he never slowed up," said Sewell. "He could stand out there for a week and barrel it in at you."

Grove's fastball had almost no tail to it. Because it was so quick to the plate, it didn't have time to do anything else. Still, it didn't make it any easier for hitters.

"Sure, we knew what was coming," said Sewell. "So what?"

That's what makes Grove's statistics so revealing. Throwing basically one pitch, here is some of what he accomplished: He won 20 or more games seven years in a row and led the league in strikeouts seven years in a row. There probably isn't a more important statistic for pitchers than earned run average. You can't always control wins, but the best pitchers give up the least runs. Grove won a record nine ERA titles. The players closest to him were Warren Spahn, Sandy Koufax, and Walter Johnson, all with five. Even more incredible was the fact that his home ballparks in Philadelphia and Boston were two hitters' parks with short fences. Left-handers still hate pitching in Fenway, with that huge wall in shallow left field that beckons to right-hand batters, "C'mon, hit me. It's easy."

Grove was raised in coal-mining country in western Maryland. Everyone in his family worked the mines, even

Grove—for two weeks. He hated the work. "I didn't put it in there, so I don't see why I have to take it out," he said.

Instead, he moved to Martinsburg, West Virginia, where he joined a semipro baseball team. It was an easier job than coal mining, and it paid better, too. Then the Martinsburg club built a new park, and to finance its new outfield fence, it sold Grove for $3,500 to the Baltimore Orioles of the International League. Grove stayed with the Orioles for five years. Grove was actually ready for the majors long before then, but the team's owner refused to sell his star to a major league club until the price was right. Only when the bidding passed $100,000 did he agree to move the 25-year-old to the Philadelphia Athletics. Who knows how many more games Grove would have won had he been allowed to join the A's earlier.

Grove led the league in strikeouts his rookie year and in ERA his sophomore season. It took him three years to win 20 in a season. After that, he was nearly unhittable until his arm injury in 1934.

When Grove was at his peak, from 1928 to 1933, he won 152 games while losing 41, for a winning percentage of .788. In Christy Mathewson's best six years, from 1903 to 1908, he won more games—177—but also lost more—69—for a winning percentage of .720. Mathewson's ERA was lower than Grove's, but ERAs were generally lower in Mathewson's day. More important, during his peak, Grove won four ERA titles. Mathewson won two.

Koufax's peak numbers were closer to Grove's. From 1961 to 1966, his winning percentage was .733. Koufax won five straight ERA titles during that period. The difference between Koufax and Grove, though, was that Grove won four more ERA titles and 135 more games than Koufax. Grove also had a better lifetime winning percentage than Koufax, .680 to .655.

Grove's best season was 1931, when he went 31-4, for a winning percentage of .886. In the four games he lost, the scores were 7-5, 4-3, 2-1, and 1-0. He not only led the league in wins and winning percentage but also in ERA, complete games, strikeouts, and shutouts. His 2.06 ERA was a full half a run lower than the second-place finisher, Lefty Gomez. They were the only two pitchers with ERAs under 3.00 that season.

In Walter Johnson's best season, he led the majors with a 1.14 ERA. That seems like a much more impressive number, except when you consider that four other pitchers had ERAs under 2.00 that year.

When his arm was sound, Grove would rear back and almost touch the ground with his knuckles before coming over the top and whipping the ball toward the plate. After he tore a muscle in his right arm in 1934, he was forced to change his style. He mastered the curve and learned pin-point control. He could no longer be called a thrower. Now he was a pitcher. He won 20 games again in 1935 and even with a sore arm, he still won four more ERA crowns.

He also loosened up a little, although not much. Once he was asked what was his funniest experience during a game, and he replied, "I never saw anything funny on a baseball field."

One of his teammates during his last few years was Hall of Famer Ted Williams, another very serious player. "He was a tantrum thrower like me," Williams said of Grove, "but when he punched a locker or something he always did it with his right hand. He was a careful tantrum thrower."

More numbers

Grove had eight seasons where his winning percentage was over .700. An outstanding reliever as well, he had 55 lifetime saves. He was 4-2 in three World Series with a 1.75 ERA. His lifetime .680 winning percentage is fourth all-time. He won 20 or more games eight times.

Throwing Strikes

His nine ERA titles are an amazing accomplishment. He also dominated the league when it came to wins, winning percentage, and strikeouts. What else is there?

Throwing Balls

Other great pitchers won more games.

Carl Owen Hubbell (King Carl, The Meal Ticket)

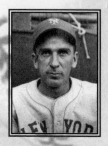

b. June 22, 1903, Carthage, Missouri
d. November 21, 1988, Scottsdale, Arizona
Career: 1928–1943
Record: 253-154
Left-handed

Sometimes people make decisions that are as flat-out wrong as, well, as the people who said the Earth was flat. Carl Hubbell could tell you all about that.

In 1925, as a 22-year-old rookie with the Detroit Tigers, he was throwing a strange pitch while warming up in the bull pen. Unlike a curve ball, this pitch broke away from right-handed batters and in on left-handers. "Well, that's the screwiest damn pitch I ever saw," his catcher said, giving what was really an old pitch a new name—the screwball.

But Hubbell's pitching coach wasn't impressed. "You're going to tear your arm up," he told him. "Don't throw that."

So Hubbell didn't for three years, and he was so ineffective that the Tigers released him to the lowly Texas League.

But sometimes fate intercedes, and that's what happened on a scalding August day in Houston, Texas, in 1928. The Democratic convention was in town. One of the delegates was Dick Kinsella, who also happened to be a scout for the New York Giants. Bored with the proceedings and overheated in the sweltering building, Kinsella went out for a walk and found himself at the ballpark, where he witnessed Hubbell pitch an 11-inning shutout for Beaumont. Kinsella called up the Giants' skipper, John McGraw, excitedly telling him he had found the team's new ace.

He was right. Hubbell became the National League's most dominating pitcher of the 1930s. Although he didn't pitch in the majors until he was 25, he still won 253 games, all for the Giants. And on one thrilling afternoon in 1934, King Carl put on a show in the all-star game the likes of which have never been seen since.

Almost as soon as Hubbell arrived on the scene, National League hitters found out that his screwball was nearly unhittable. Pitching in relief against the Cardinals shortly after he joined the Giants in 1928, Hubbell faced future Hall of Famer Chick Hafey. Catcher Shanty Hogan signaled Hubbell for a fastball, but instead, Hubbell tossed his screwball. Hafey swung and missed, so Hubbell threw him another one, striking him out. Hogan called time and headed out to the mound. "I don't know what that pitch was," he said to the rookie, "but keep throwing it."

Hubbell mastered the screwball better than anyone else, but he didn't invent it. Christy Mathewson, who learned it himself from another pitcher, was using it to baffle hitters at the turn of the century, but he called it "the fadeaway." But while Mathewson also had a blazing fastball, Hubbell's speed was ordinary, so he was forced to rely mostly on the screwball. In fact, Hubbell threw it so often that his left arm eventually became permanently twisted.

To Hubbell it was worth it. He won 20 games five years in a row. In three of those years, he also captured the ERA crown. In 1933, when he led the league with a 1.66 ERA, no one else was under 2.00. His lifetime ERA was 2.98, the lowest among pitchers who were active through most of the decade. Lefty Grove, the American League's most dominating pitcher of the 1930s, had a lifetime ERA of 3.06. Hubbell's great rival in the National League, Dizzy Dean, owned a 3.02 lifetime ERA.

Opponents hit .253 against Dean, .255 against Grove, and .251 against Hubbell. Both Grove and Dean gave up 8.8 hits per game; Hubbell, 8.7.

Hubbell also had incredible stamina. On July 2, 1933, he took the mound against the Cardinals and that day pitched maybe one of the best games in baseball history—an 18-inning, 1-0 victory. He gave up only six hits, four of them scratch hits. He did not walk a single batter and struck out 12. Twelve of the 18 innings he pitched were perfect.

But it was at the 1934 all-star game that Hubbell really demonstrated his mastery. It was a performance that is still the benchmark for all great all-star performances. What made it especially incredible was that every starter for the American League was a future Hall of Famer. There has never been a more powerful lineup. Yet they bowed meekly to King Carl.

Charlie Gehringer, the Detroit Tigers' second baseman, opened the game with a single off Hubbell, who then walked the next batter, Heinie Manush. The National League catcher Gabby Hartnett called time and approached the mound. "Come on, Hub, throw that thing," he said, referring to the screwball. "Hell, I can't hit it, and they can't either."

What followed was one of the most amazing pitching exhibitions ever seen on the diamond. Up to the plate stepped Babe Ruth, maybe the most fearsome hitter of all time. The Babe was past his prime but still dangerous. Hubbell struck him out looking, on four pitches. Ruth never even took the bat off his shoulder. Lou Gehrig followed. He fanned on four pitches, looking foolish as he helplessly swatted at strike three. Jimmie Foxx, the Philadelphia Athletics' fearsome slugger, was Hubbell's next victim. He swung and missed at three screwballs, although he did manage a foul tip on one pitch. That ended the inning.

But Hubbell wasn't done. Leading off the next inning was Al Simmons, followed by Joe Cronin. Both went down on strikes. Five Hall of Fame sluggers, five strikeouts. Hubbell added one more when American League pitcher Lefty Gomez went down swinging, giving Gomez, a career .147 hitter, something to boast about the rest of his life: "That day, I was as good as the greatest hitters ever."

Amazingly, long after he retired, Hubbell would say that game wasn't his best. Instead, he preferred to recall a one-hitter he threw against the Dodgers in 1940, when he faced the minimum 27 hitters (the lone successful batter was retired on a double play), throwing only 81 pitches over nine innings.

"He didn't really have overpowering stuff, but he was an absolute master of what he did have," said fellow Hall of Famer Billy Herman. "I never saw another pitcher who could so fascinate the opposition the way Hubbell did."

In the beginning of his career, Hubbell was called "The Meal Ticket," meaning that when he went to the mound you were pretty much assured of a good meal—or in this case, a win. That was literally true, beginning in July 1936, when Hubbell shutout the Pirates to lift his record to 11-6 on the season. He won a total of 16 straight games till the end of the season, as he guided the Giants to the National League pennant. He led the league that year in wins (26), winning percentage (.813), and ERA (2.31). In 1937, he picked up where he left off, running up eight more wins in a row until his streak was finally snapped on Memorial Day. His 24 straight victories remain a major league record.

More Numbers

Hubbell is the only pitcher in major league history to win two Most Valuable Player awards during peacetime (1933, 1936). (Hal Newhouser won it twice when talent was diluted during World War II.) He led the league in wins three times and in winning percentage twice. In the 1933 World Series, Hubbell pitched 20 innings, surrendering no runs to the Washington Senators, whose .287 team average led the majors. His ERA in three Series appearances was 1.79. He was elected to the Hall of Fame in 1947, his first year of eligibility.

Throwing Strikes

Hubbell dominated hitters in a decade when hitters had the upper hand against pitchers. At his peak, he and his screwball owned the greatest hitters of all time. Had he been permitted to throw it earlier, he could easily have won 300 games.

Throwing Balls

Although he led the league in strikeouts once, he was not a strikeout pitcher. Other pitchers had a higher winning percentage.

Randall Johnson (Randy, The Big Unit)

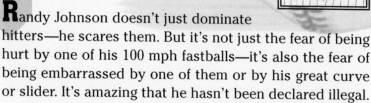

b. September 10, 1963, Walnut Creek,
  California
Career: 1988–
Left-handed

Randy Johnson doesn't just dominate hitters—he scares them. But it's not just the fear of being hurt by one of his 100 mph fastballs—it's also the fear of being embarrassed by one of them or by his great curve or slider. It's amazing that he hasn't been declared illegal.

Johnson is 6 feet 10 inches tall with arms so long he can change stations on a car radio from the backseat. Imagine what it's like to look up at him from home plate, standing on a mound that is already 10 inches above field level.

"Johnson's so tall, sometimes it seemed like he was just handing the ball to our catcher," said his former teammate Ken Griffey, Jr.

Johnson has always been tall, and he's always had incredible stuff, but it wasn't until his 30th birthday that he learned to harness it. Until then, his won-lost record was an average 49-48, but since then he has gone 175-58 for an incredible .751 winning percentage.

What happened when he turned 30? Something terrible. Johnson had always been very close to his father, who was very supportive of him and had spent hours upon hours with Randy when he was a youngster, helping him develop as a pitcher. But on Christmas day 1992, his father died suddenly of a heart attack. Randy was devastated. At first, he decided to retire from baseball, but his mother and his girlfriend convinced him that he should stay in the game to honor his father's memory.

"From that day on, I got a lot more strength and determination to be the best player I could be, and not to get sidetracked and not to look at things as pressure but as challenges," Johnson said.

The change in attitude was obviously a big help, but Johnson's mechanics needed work as well. While being 6 feet 10 inches tall has its advantages (he is the tallest pitcher in major league history), being that height can also hinder a pitcher, because it's more difficult to coordinate your movements. One day in 1992 when Johnson was still struggling in Seattle, the Mariners were playing the Texas Rangers. In the Rangers' bull pen, Nolan Ryan and the Rangers' pitching coach, Tom House, were noticing Johnson's control problems. Afterward, they talked to him. Ryan suggested that Johnson improve his follow-through by driving toward the plate efficiently. House, meanwhile, talked to Johnson about being more mentally tough.

It took awhile, but the lessons eventually sank in. Johnson struck out 308 batters in 1993. He has since struck out more than 300 hitters in a season five more times, from 1998 to 2002. Five consecutive years of more than 300 is unmatched by any other pitcher. Only Ryan has ever struck out 300 hitters three years in a row. But it's almost unfair to compare the two. Johnson's winning percentage lifetime is .679. Ryan's is .526. Although Ryan struck out many more batters than Johnson, Johnson's ratio of strikeouts per nine innings is higher, 11.21 to 9.55. Among active pitchers, Johnson's winning percentage is second only to Pedro Martinez's, but Johnson has also pitched many more years than Martinez. His strikeouts per nine innings ratio is higher than Martinez's, and Johnson also has more than twice as many career shutouts, 34 to 15.

Johnson is also a more durable pitcher than Martinez. Over the course of his career, Martinez has averaged 189 innings a season; Johnson has averaged 201.

When most people talk about Johnson, they speak in awe of his 100 mph fastball, and deservedly so, but it's the slider, which is thrown 10 miles an hour slower, that makes him so devastating. Imagine the poor batter who is so eager to get a head start on the fastball, so he begins his swing early—only to get the slider. By the time he has finished swinging, the slider is just approaching the plate.

It's also Johnson's motion that makes him so hard to hit—especially for left-handed hitters. It looks as if his arm is coming at them from the right-field stands.

"His arm angle and velocity force you to commit to his pitch long before it's on you. And when it is on you, it's usually between your feet—and you've still swung," says Johnson's stablemate, Curt Schilling.

It's a double trap, because if hitters wait on the slider, they get the supersonic heater. Only Johnson can make a 100 mph fastball appear even quicker than it is. No wonder he has just about owned most major league hitters the last 10 years. In 2002, Johnson captured his fourth straight Cy Young Award and his fifth overall, one short of Roger Clemens, although Clemens has never won four in a row. Greg Maddux has also won four in a row, but Johnson has kept hitters to a lower batting average than Maddux, .212 to .242, and Johnson's lifetime winning percentage of .679 is higher than Maddux's .642.

In 2001, Johnson and Schilling basically carried the Diamondbacks on their backs, leading the team to its first world championship. Johnson led the majors in strikeouts for the eighth time. His 13.4 strikeouts per nine innings was a major league record. He also earned his second ERA title in three seasons. He topped it off with five wins in the postseason and three in the World Series against the Yankees.

In 2002, he was even better. This time, he took the league's triple crown for pitchers, leading the league in wins, (with 24) ERA, and strikeouts. In his last 13 starts, he was 11-1. Will he ever get old?

More numbers

Johnson's 3,746 career strikeouts are fourth all-time. He co-owns the major league record (along with Roger Clemens and Kerry Wood) for strikeouts in a game with 20. He has struck out 19 batters in a game twice.

Throwing Strikes

He is not only one of the game's all-time strikeout artists, he is also a winner, as his outstanding won-lost percentage and his five Cy Young Awards demonstrate.

Throwing Balls

It took him many years to become a great pitcher. He is a very poor fielder.

Walter Perry Johnson (The Big Train)

b. November 6, 1887, Humboldt, Kansas
d. December 10, 1946, Washington, D.C.
Career: 1907–1927
Record: 417-279
Right-handed

They didn't have radar guns in Walter Johnson's day, so we'll never know how fast he really was. Instead, we have to rely on the accounts of the poor hitters who had to face him for 20 years, sometimes trembling in fear for their lives.

The first thing that people always noticed about Johnson was his arms. They weren't like anyone else's. They nearly reached his knees. His long limbs created a whiplike action so when he released the ball in his easy, sidearmed—almost underhand—motion, the ball would rocket toward the plate and announce its arrival with a *swoosh* that could be heard in the stands.

By the time the hitter thought he was getting a look at it, it had already slammed into the catcher's mitt.

"You can't hit it if you can't see it," said the Yankees' Ping Bodie, speaking for the rest of the American League.

They couldn't hit it even when they knew it was coming. For the first 15 years of his career, if the hitters guessed fastball, most of the time they were right. But it's a tribute to Johnson's incredible speed that he won over 400 games without any trickery, just raw, blatant power.

"Gosh, if he had had a curve, he would never have lost a game," said Donie Bush, who batted against Johnson many times.

He also might not have lost a game if he had played for a decent team. There was a saying about George Washington: "First in war, first in peace, and first in the hearts of his countrymen." About the Senators, fans joked: "First in war, first in peace, and last in the American League." It was nearly true. Johnson played 18 years for the Washington Senators before they made it to the World Series. He was with the Nationals (the team's nickname) six years before they rose above seventh place in an eight-team league.

Speaking of George Washington, do you know that story about him tossing a silver dollar across the Rappahannock River? It takes a pretty good arm to do that. Many tried but couldn't come close. In 1936, nine years after Johnson retired, the city decided to commemmorate the 204th anniversary of Washington's birth and asked Johnson to throw a silver dollar across the river. He flung the silver dollar 372 feet, easily making it to the opposite shore.

Johnson's 110 shutouts are first all-time (by a wide margin), but he just about had to pitch a shutout to win. In his career, he pitched in 54 1-0 games and lost 26 of them. In one game, he retired 28 Yankees in a row over 10 innings and didn't win. Still, he led the league in wins six times in his career, including four years in a row, from 1913 to 1916. He won 20 or more games for 10 straight years, from 1910 to 1919.

"Of course, the greatest of them all was Walter Johnson," said Hall of Famer Sam Crawford in Lawrence Ritter's *The Glory of Their Times.* "He was the best I ever faced, without a doubt."

Jimmy Austin, another old-timer interviewed by Ritter, echoed Crawford. "Lefty Grove was fast, and Sandy Koufax is, too. But you should have seen Walter Johnson. On a cloudy day, you couldn't see the ball half the time, it came in so fast."

Even as a child, Johnson exhibited unusual hand-eye coordination. His brother, Earl, recalled that young Walt could hit a squirrel from 60 feet away with a slingshot. When some bigger boys refused to let him pitch in their game, saying he was too small, he amazed them by grabbing the ball and tossing it with all his might. Unfortunately, it smashed through the biggest window in the school.

For a while, he was a catcher. Then he was sent in to pitch in a losing game. He proceeded to strike out 12 youngsters and learned right there that pitching and winning gave him more pleasure than anything.

"From the first time I held a ball, it settled in the palm of my right hand as though it belonged there, and when I threw it, ball, hand and wrist, arm and shoulder and back seemed to all work together," he recalled.

His speed was obvious to anyone who stepped in against him—and so was his lack of control, so he worked at that. He would walk around town with his wagon in tow and gather up as many empty cans as he could find. Then he would line them up and throw rocks at them over and over again from 90 feet away. Did it help? For a fastballer, Johnson developed remarkable control. He averaged only 2.1 walks a game and he never once led the league in walks, in contrast to players such as Amos Rusie, Bob Feller, and Nolan Ryan, all of whom had fastballs that were compared to Johnson's. Rusie led the league in walks five times in his nine full seasons. Feller was a four-time walk leader, averaging 4.1 a game during his career. Ryan led the league eight times and ranks first all-time in walks issued.

Johnson starred for his high school team and as a semipro pitcher, but because he was playing out in Idaho at a time when baseball was concentrated in the East, and there was no radio or television to broadcast his exploits, no major league teams knew about him. A local scout did, though, and he sent letter after letter about Johnson to Joe Cantillon, the Senators' manager. Cantillon threw the letters away until one caught his eye. It read, "This boy throws so fast you can't see 'em, and he knows where he is throwing, because if he didn't there would be dead bodies all over Idaho."

Cantillon knew of another player in the area he wanted to scout, so he dispatched an injured catcher named Cliff Blankenship to take a look, telling him to check out this Johnson fellow if he had the time. Blankenship took one glimpse at Johnson on the mound and knew he was the real thing.

Johnson started 12 games for the Nats the summer of 1907, winning only five, but with an ERA of 1.87. It was the first of 11 years that Johnson had an ERA below 2.00. Christy Mathewson did it six times, as did Grover Cleveland Alexander.

In 1909, Johnson's record was 13-25, but that only tells you how bad the Senators were. He was second in the league in strikeouts, third in innings, and fourth in complete games.

In 1910, he led the league in strikeouts for the first of a major league record 12 times. (Ryan was first for 11 seasons.) When he retired in 1927, he was the only pitcher in major league history to have recorded more than 3,000 strikeouts. His 3,508 strikeouts remained the record until it was passed by Nolan Ryan in 1983. Most of Johnson's strikeouts were achieved in the Dead Ball Era, when players choked up on the bat and sought mostly to put the ball in play rather than in the seats. That meant strikeout numbers were much lower in Johnson's day than they were in Ryan's. Had Johnson been pitching today, there's no doubt his total would have been higher.

ending his career with a poor ball club.
for the Yankees, for example, his numbers
en in the stratosphere. He didn't just win
inated them, as his strikeout and shutout
rate.

Balls

s are fourth all-time.

Casey Stengel, who gained most of his fame as manager of the Yankees and Mets, played against Johnson. For years he loved to tell about the experience. "Johnson made a pitching motion. The ump called strike. I stood there," Casey recalled. "The same thing happened on strike two. When Walter rocked his arm again, I threw my bat away and went back to the bench. 'Come back here, you blind fathead,' the ump yelled. 'He threw that last ball to first base.'

"'That's all right,' I yelled from the bench, 'cuz I didn't see the other two either.'"

Johnson was at his best in 1912 and 1913, when he won 33 and 36 games respectively. In 1913, he held American League hitters to a .187 batting average. His 1.14 ERA set a record for right-handers that wasn't broken until Bob Gibson lowered it in 1968 to 1.12. Actually, Johnson should still be holding the record. On the last day of the season, the Senators fielded a team of substitutes and old-timers. Johnson, who played outfield most of the game, went in to pitch to two hitters and just lobbed the ball over the plate. When those two runners scored, it raised Johnson's season ERA from 1.09 to 1.14.

In 1913, he hurled 55⅔ consecutive scoreless innings, which remained a major league record until it was surpassed by Don Drysdale in 1968, the year when hitters fared so poorly at the plate that Carl Yastrzemski was the only American League hitter to top .300.

Because of his great speed, the gentlemanly Johnson was terrified of hitting and killing a batter, so he never threw directly at a player. When he did hit someone, he would become so upset he'd be ineffective on the mound. After Johnson nearly killed a player accidentally in 1915, Ty Cobb took advantage of Johnson's fear and began crowding the plate with great success, knowing that

Johnson would never brush him back.

Not surprisingly, Johnson was also one of the most beloved players ever to grace the diamond. His teammate Joe Judge liked to tell the story about the evening that the two of them were late for a movie because Johnson was engaged in a conversation with a fan. Finally, Johnson and the fan shook hands and parted. As they entered the theater, Judge asked Johnson what took so long, and Johnson replied, "The man said he knew my sister in Kansas."

When Judge said he didn't know that Johnson had a sister, the pitcher answered, "I don't."

In 1924, the Senators finally finished in first place, and the whole nation seemed to cheer the good fortune of the beloved Big Train, who at 36 was getting his first chance at postseason play. But at first it did not look as if it was heading toward a storybook ending for Johnson. He pitched well but lost 4-3 in 12 innings in Game 1. Perhaps tired from that long stint, he pitched poorly in Game 5 and lost again. In Game 7, the score was tied, 3-3, when the Nats' manager, Bucky Harris, signaled to the bull pen and brought in Johnson to start the eighth. The game went into extra innings with Johnson at the helm. Though he was in trouble in nearly every inning, he managed to call on his fastball when he needed it and he kept the Giants in check until the Senators pushed a run across in the 12th inning for the victory—and the world championship.

The Senators finished in first place again in 1925. This time, Johnson pitched brilliantly in his first two starts, winning twice. But Game 7 was played in a virtual downpour, and Johnson was unable to get any footing in the ankle-deep mud on the mound. He surrendered five

earned runs, as
take the series.

Two years lat
bat of one of his tea
shattered his leg.
he couldn't get the
Over the years, he
ting practice or a co
The young players w
effortless underhand
the batter's box, expe
old guy, when sudden
Johnson *swoosh!* Then
mouthed amazement.

Even in his early 50s
running at full speed.

More numbers

Johnson's 417 wins are seco
a five-time leader in ERA. (
2.17 ERA is seventh all-time.
seven times, tying him with
He is fifth in complete games
among pitchers who played sol
5,924 innings pitched are third.

Throwing strikes

Maybe the fastest pitcher in basel
in more categories than any othe

games while sp
Had he pitched
would have be
games, he don
totals demons

Throwing

His 279 losse

Adrian Joss (Addie)

b. April 12, 1880, Woodland, Wisconsin
d. April 14, 1911, Toledo, Ohio
Career: 1902–1911
Record: 160-97
Right-handed

When old-timers talked about Addie Joss, two stories were always told. The first was the incredible game he pitched against Big Ed Walsh to keep the Cleveland Indians in the race at the end of the 1908 season. Indeed, many fans believe the two put on the finest pitching performance in baseball history. The second thing they remembered, with tears in their eyes, was how this amazing talent and one of the most decent men ever to don a baseball uniform died tragically at the age of 31.

Addie's ability to throw a baseball harder than most people became apparent when he was a young boy. While tossing a ball against a solid brick wall on his aunt and uncle's farm, he shattered one of the bricks. Instead of being angry at their nephew, they encouraged him and for years they proudly pointed out the damage to visitors as a historic marker of Joss's great talent.

Addie first played organized ball on his town team. He quickly demonstrated an overwhelming fastball, a sharp curve, and a bewildering change of pace. The pitches were made all the more difficult to hit by Joss's unusual delivery. During his windup, he would make an almost complete about-face so that, for an instant, he faced second base. Then he would swivel back and go into a high kick before delivering a well-hidden ball to the plate. Awkward as it might sound, it was a very practical motion. After the pitch, Joss's feet were square to home, ready to field the ball on either side of the mound. As a result, Joss was regarded as the premier fielder among major league pitchers of his day.

Joss did not make a quiet appearance in the majors. His first game on April 26, 1902, was a one-hit shutout that would have been a no-hitter if not for what observers agreed was an umpire's blown call.

During his nine-year career, Joss never had the opportunity to play for a great team, but four years in a row, from 1905 to 1908, he won 20 or more games. An even more important pitching statistic than wins is ERA. A mediocre pitcher with a lot of run support can still win 20 games. He can give up five runs a game, but if his team gets six runs, they win. Joss's highest ERA from 1905 to 1908 was 2.01. His highest ERA in his entire career was only 2.77.

Joss won two ERA titles and finished among the top five six times—more than half his career. By contrast, Tom Seaver, whose 2.86 was one of the lowest of the modern era, finished among the top five in ERA seven times in 20 years, or slightly more than one third of his career.

Only Ed Walsh had a lower lifetime ERA, by seven one-hundredths of a point, 1.82 to Joss's 1.89. In third place is Mordecai Brown with a 2.06. Joss also had terrific control, giving up only 1.41 walks per game, good enough for 13th all-time. Walsh, his great rival, is 44th on the all-time list with 1.87 walks per game.

Joss and Walsh will always be compared with each other, if only for that one dramatic afternoon in 1908 when the two rivals faced off and produced a masterpiece.

Coming into the game, Cleveland and Walsh's White Sox were in a neck-and-neck battle for the pennant. The spitballing Walsh, a future Hall of Famer, was enjoying what would be the best year of his career. In 1908, he would lead the league with 40 wins. But in Joss, Walsh was

Casey Stengel, who gained most of his fame as manager of the Yankees and Mets, played against Johnson. For years he loved to tell about the experience. "Johnson made a pitching motion. The ump called strike. I stood there," Casey recalled. "The same thing happened on strike two. When Walter rocked his arm again, I threw my bat away and went back to the bench. 'Come back here, you blind fathead,' the ump yelled. 'He threw that last ball to first base.'

"'That's all right,' I yelled from the bench, 'cuz I didn't see the other two either.'"

Johnson was at his best in 1912 and 1913, when he won 33 and 36 games respectively. In 1913, he held American League hitters to a .187 batting average. His 1.14 ERA set a record for right-handers that wasn't broken until Bob Gibson lowered it in 1968 to 1.12. Actually, Johnson should still be holding the record. On the last day of the season, the Senators fielded a team of substitutes and old-timers. Johnson, who played outfield most of the game, went in to pitch to two hitters and just lobbed the ball over the plate. When those two runners scored, it raised Johnson's season ERA from 1.09 to 1.14.

In 1913, he hurled 55⅔ consecutive scoreless innings, which remained a major league record until it was surpassed by Don Drysdale in 1968, the year when hitters fared so poorly at the plate that Carl Yastrzemski was the only American League hitter to top .300.

Because of his great speed, the gentlemanly Johnson was terrified of hitting and killing a batter, so he never threw directly at a player. When he did hit someone, he would become so upset he'd be ineffective on the mound. After Johnson nearly killed a player accidentally in 1915, Ty Cobb took advantage of Johnson's fear and began crowding the plate with great success, knowing that

Johnson would never brush him back.

Not surprisingly, Johnson was also one of the most beloved players ever to grace the diamond. His teammate Joe Judge liked to tell the story about the evening that the two of them were late for a movie because Johnson was engaged in a conversation with a fan. Finally, Johnson and the fan shook hands and parted. As they entered the theater, Judge asked Johnson what took so long, and Johnson replied, "The man said he knew my sister in Kansas."

When Judge said he didn't know that Johnson had a sister, the pitcher answered, "I don't."

In 1924, the Senators finally finished in first place, and the whole nation seemed to cheer the good fortune of the beloved Big Train, who at 36 was getting his first chance at postseason play. But at first it did not look as if it was heading toward a storybook ending for Johnson. He pitched well but lost 4-3 in 12 innings in Game 1. Perhaps tired from that long stint, he pitched poorly in Game 5 and lost again. In Game 7, the score was tied, 3-3, when the Nats' manager, Bucky Harris, signaled to the bull pen and brought in Johnson to start the eighth. The game went into extra innings with Johnson at the helm. Though he was in trouble in nearly every inning, he managed to call on his fastball when he needed it and he kept the Giants in check until the Senators pushed a run across in the 12th inning for the victory—and the world championship.

The Senators finished in first place again in 1925. This time, Johnson pitched brilliantly in his first two starts, winning twice. But Game 7 was played in a virtual downpour, and Johnson was unable to get any footing in the ankle-deep mud on the mound. He surrendered five earned runs, as Pittsburgh defeated Washington, 9-7, to take the series.

Two years later, Johnson was hit by a line drive off the bat of one of his teammates during spring training. The smash shattered his leg. Though he returned later in the season, he couldn't get the same push off his foot and he retired. Over the years, he would periodically return to pitch batting practice or a couple of innings of an exhibition game. The young players would laugh at the old-timer with the effortless underhand motion. Then they would step into the batter's box, expecting to have to take it easy on the old guy, when suddenly they would hear the trademark Johnson *swoosh!* Then they'd stare at the mound in open-mouthed amazement.

Even in his early 50s, The Big Train's engine was still running at full speed.

More numbers

Johnson's 417 wins are second to Cy Young's 511. He was a five-time leader in ERA. (Young led twice.) His lifetime 2.17 ERA is seventh all-time. He led the league in shutouts seven times, tying him with Grover Cleveland Alexander. He is fifth in complete games with 531, which is the most among pitchers who played solely in the 20th century. His 5,924 innings pitched are third.

Throwing strikes

Maybe the fastest pitcher in baseball history, Johnson led in more categories than any other pitcher. He won 417 games while spending his career with a poor ball club. Had he pitched for the Yankees, for example, his numbers would have been in the stratosphere. He didn't just win games, he dominated them, as his strikeout and shutout totals demonstrate.

Throwing Balls

His 279 losses are fourth all-time.

facing the league's leader in earned run average. The game had the kind of buildup usually reserved for championship fights. Every baseball fan in 1908 knew that this would be the game of the year.

The two didn't disappoint. In the third inning, the Naps (the team's nickname, after manager Napoleon Lajoie) pushed a run against Walsh, but the Sox had no such luck against Joss, who quickly set down every batter who approached the plate. In the eighth, Lajoie skillfully handled a bad hop at second, and in the ninth, third baseman Bill Bradley snared a drive down the line. When he made the long throw to first, the Indians won, 1-0. Walsh had set an American League record, striking out 15 while surrendering four hits. But Joss was better. In a game he had to win, Joss delivered a perfect game, only the second in the history of the American League. His control was so sharp, he needed only 74 pitches to retire all 27 White Sox hitters.

Though Cleveland came a half game shy of winning the pennant, it wasn't Joss's fault. Through September and October, he was 7-1. His 1.16 ERA that season led the league. In 325 innings, he walked only 30 batters, less than one a game.

In 1910, an elbow injury threatened to end his career, but he was determined to come back in 1911, when he suddenly collapsed during spring training. He was taken to the hospital. He had meningitis, and there was no cure. On April 14, he died.

Joss was beloved by his teammates and opponents alike.

"Most people will think of Addie Joss as a great baseball player, one of the greatest of his time," said Toledo Mayor Brand Whitlock. "While he was that, and that is a big thing to be, he was much more than that. He was as good a man as he was a pitcher, as good a husband, as good a father, as good a friend, as good a citizen."

Joss left behind a wife and two children. To help them out, the best players in baseball on their own gathered together on July 24 for a game, with all the receipts going to the Joss family. It was the first all-star game ever played.

Joss played only nine seasons, and it takes ten to qualify for the Hall of Fame. But in 1978, the Hall made an exception, and Joss was elected. That's how good he was.

More Numbers

He had four 20-win seasons during his nine years. He pitched two no-hitters, seven one-hitters, and had 45 shutouts. He rarely had a bad outing and had terrific endurance, completing 234 of the 260 games he started.

Throwing Strikes

He pitched maybe the finest pressure game in baseball history. His ERA is the second lowest of all time.

Throwing Balls

His career was not very long. His winning percentage of .623 was lower than that of others.

Timothy John Keefe (Smiling Tim, Sir Timothy)

b. January 1, 1857, Cambridge, Massachusetts
d. April 23, 1933, Cambridge, Massachusetts
Career: 1880–1893
Record: 342-225
Right-handed

Few pitches can make a batter look as silly as a well-thrown change of pace. The pitcher rears back and grunts before whipping his arm forward as hard as he can. The batter, expecting a fastball, swings almost as soon as the ball leaves the pitcher's hand. The only problem is, even after the batter has completed his swing, the ball is still taking its own sweet time, stopping for coffee and a newspaper on its way to the catcher's mitt. Ever seen a human corkscrew? That's a hitter who has just swung helplessly at a change of pace.

The man who perfected the pitch was Tim Keefe, who was so good at it that people called him Sir Timothy. They called his pitch the "ice cream ball" because it had time to melt on its way to home plate.

The key to the change of pace is in the grip. By holding the ball in the palm instead of the fingers, the ball doesn't spring from the hands with the velocity of a fastball, even though the arm motion is the same. Armed with this new pitch, Keefe became a star almost immediately. In fact, his .86 ERA as a rookie for Troy in 1880 is the major league record for 19th-century hurlers.

Keefe came to the majors after playing amateur baseball around his hometown of Cambridge, Massachusetts. He was a man of unusual character. Decent and quiet off the mound, he was a far cry from the ruffians who dominated the game in the 19th century. Keefe was such a sensitive person that after he hit an opposing batter in the temple with a fastball in 1887, he suffered a nervous breakdown and missed several weeks of the season. Maybe he inherited some of his principles from his father, a Northerner who found himself in the South when the Civil War broke out. Rather than serve in the Confederate army, he spent three years in prison.

Even at the peak of his success, Keefe was smart enough to know his baseball career could end at any moment, so he taught himself shorthand in case he needed an alternative career. As it turned out, his shorthand lengthened his baseball career. He was one of the first pitchers to take meticulous notes—all in shorthand—on the tendencies of opposing hitters and then use that information on the mound. He was also one of the first great strategists. He figured out he could be more effective by pitching tight to hitters who crowded the plate and outside to those who stood back in the batter's box.

It worked, too. He won more than 30 games a season six years in a row. Twice during that streak he topped 40 wins. He won 342 games over 14 seasons, eighth all-time and an average of 24 wins a season, even though for several years he was plagued by playing for terrible teams. From that period, only Pud Galvin had more wins with 361. But Keefe's 2.62 lifetime ERA was lower than Galvin's. It also topped Charley "Old Hoss" Radbourn's and John Clarkson's, his two other great rivals from that era.

Mickey Welch, his teammate on the New York Giants and another great pitcher of the era, greatly admired Keefe. "I never saw a pitcher better than Keefe. It is true that he was most effective at the old distance of fifty feet. But if he had been a modern pitcher at 60 feet 6 inches, he would have had no superior. He was a master strategist who knew the weakness of every batter in the league. I'd put him in the class of Hoss Radbourn and John Clarkson."

In 1888, Keefe won 19 straight games, a record that stood alone until it was tied by Rube Marquard in 1912. The difference was that Keefe needed only six weeks to win his 19. It took Marquard more than three months.

In 1883, Keefe started 68 games and completed them all, pitching 619 innings while winning 41 games. That season, he led the league in fewest hits per game with 7.1. His 361 strikeouts also led the league. He would top 300 strikeouts three times in his career, a record that stood until it was broken by Nolan Ryan nearly 100 years later.

On July 4, he pitched the first game of a doubleheader, winning a one-hitter. Then he came back and tossed a two-hitter to win the nightcap.

His best season was 1888, when he led the league in wins with 35 and winning percentage with .745, gave up the fewest hits per game, and led the league in strikeouts and ERA. That fall, he pitched four games and won three, as the Giants defeated the Browns of the American Association in the World Series. The next year, he won the last game of the season, which gave the Giants another National League championship. He then won two games over the Brooklyn Bridegrooms as the New Yorkers claimed their second championship in a row.

More Numbers

Keefe twice led the league in wins, three times in ERA. Radbourn and Clarkson led the league in this important category only once. Galvin never did. Four times Keefe surrendered the fewest hits per game, and five times he kept opposing hitters to the lowest batting average.

Throwing Strikes

He was one of the great thinkers and strategists on the mound and would have figured out a way to succeed in any era.

Throwing Balls

His lifetime .603 winning percentage wasn't as high as other Hall of Famers. Others averaged more wins per season.

Sanford Koufax (Sandy)

b. December 30, 1935, Brooklyn, New York
Career: 1955–1966
Record: 165-87
Left-handed

Sandy Koufax was a great mystery in his early years with the Dodgers. Here was a young pitcher with a heater that was so fast, some called it a radio ball— you could hear it, but you couldn't see it. And he had a curve that was so sharp, it was simply unhittable. So what was the mystery? His control. He had none. When Koufax was pitching, people watching the game from behind home plate needed batting helmets.

Then one day during spring training in 1961, Dodger catcher Norm Sherry had an idea. "You have the best fastball in the game," he told Koufax, who, after six years in the league had a mediocre record of 36-40. "Why not take some speed off of it. It will still be unhittable, but you'll be able to throw with more control."

Koufax tried it his next time out, and suddenly his pitches were regularly finding the plate. He won 18 games that year. And from 1961–1966, when he retired prematurely at 30, because of arthritis in his elbow, his record was 129-47. He was the most dominating pitcher in baseball.

"You put the whommy on him, but when he's pitchin', the whommy tends to go on vacation," said Casey Stengel about Koufax.

Although he grew up playing baseball, Koufax actually wanted to be a basketball player, and at 6 feet 2 inches tall he was a good one. But then he was offered a baseball scholarship at the University of Cincinnati. It was there that baseball scouts took notice. He had a tryout for the Giants, but they showed no interest. (Imagine a team that had Juan Marichal and Koufax in the same rotation!) The Yankees were also tempted until Koufax requested a bonus. That left the Dodgers, who signed him for $14,000 in 1955.

Unfortunately for Koufax, the bonus turned out to be a huge burden. Major league rules required that a player who signed for over $10,000 had to stay with the parent club. Koufax couldn't be sent to the minor leagues, where he could have learned his trade. Instead, he had to learn in the majors, mostly by sitting on the bench for long stretches at a time because the team couldn't risk using him while it was in a pennant race.

In 1959, he showed glimmers of his potential. On August 31, he struck out 18 Giants, tying the major league record. That fall, he started Game 5 of the World Series, losing 1-0, although he only surrendered one run and five hits in seven innings.

But 1960, when he slipped to 8-13, was a step back. He even considered quitting the game, until his sudden success in the spring of 1961. That year, pitching with his same distinctly overhand motion but staying more within himself, he captured his first strikeout title. His 269 strikeouts that season set the modern National League record for left-handers. He would win three more. He would have won five more if he hadn't lost starts to injuries in 1962 and 1964. Grove led the league in strikeouts seven times, but only once did he ever strike out more than 200 batters, when he KO'd 209 in 1930. After notching 197 in 1960, Koufax topped 200 six years in a row. Three times he struck out over 300 batters, including 1965, when he set the major league record of 382. Over the course of his career, he averaged over a strikeout an inning. Grove averaged under six a game.

Though an injury to his pitching hand cut short his 1962 season, he still won his first of five straight ERA titles, breaking a record set by Grove. Koufax also had a better lifetime ERA than Grove did—2.76 to 3.06.

In his prime, from 1927 to 1933, Grove pitched for one of the strongest teams in baseball history—the Philadelphia Athletics. The A's won three pennants and two World Series from 1929 to 1931 while batting over .290 as a team. They were led by three future Hall of Fame sluggers: Jimmie Foxx, Al Simmons, and Mickey Cochrane. Who couldn't win with that team?

While Koufax's Dodgers won three pennants and two world championships during his peak years, it was largely because of him that they did so. The Dodgers didn't hit much. Their average in 1963 was .251. Still, they swept the Yankees in the World Series. Koufax, who was 25-5 during the season, beat the Bombers twice. His 15 strikeouts in Game 1 set a World Series record. He also won Game 4, 2-1, limiting the Yankees to six hits.

"I don't see how he lost five games during the season," said Yankee great Yogi Berra.

In 1965, when the Dodgers again won the World Series, their .245 average was seventh in the league, yet Koufax finished the season 26-8, leading the league in wins, winning percentage, innings, ERA, complete games, and strikeouts. He won two games in the World Series (after refusing to pitch the opener because it fell on Yom Kippur, a Jewish holiday), including the last game, in which he shut out the Minnesota Twins, 2-0, pitching a complete-game three-hitter on only two days' rest.

In comparison to today's game, Koufax's complete-game numbers are mind-boggling. Despite suffering from arthritis in his throwing arm, a condition that would end his career a year later, he completed 27 ball games in 1965. Only twice in his career has Greg Maddux had as many as 10. Roger Clemens? His highest total was 18 in 1987. The next year he had 14. Koufax had 20 or more three times, and he threw harder than either of them.

Although he embarrassed them at the plate, opposing hitters frequently said they preferred to hit against Koufax rather than Bob Gibson or Juan Marichal. The reason was that his control was so good, and he was so dominating, he hardly ever hit anyone. (He didn't need to do it on purpose.) He even tipped off his pitches. Tim McCarver said hitters always knew what Koufax was going to throw, and Koufax himself knew that. But he didn't care, because he knew they couldn't hit him.

How great was he in comparison with pitchers of his own era? Koufax won the Cy Young Award three times, in 1963, 1965, and 1966. (Nobody doubted that in 1964 he was the best pitcher in the game. He went 19-5 that year, winning his 19th in August, but an elbow injury ended his season that month.) Roger Clemens has now won the award a record six times, but there is a huge difference. In Koufax's day the award went to the best pitcher in the game, not just in one league, as it has since 1967, the year after Koufax retired. Gibson didn't win a Cy Young until after Koufax left the game. Marichal, who was at his peak while Koufax was at his, never won one.

In his last year, Koufax's record was 27-9, but while he could still blow away hitters, he couldn't make the pain in his elbow go away. Ironically, Koufax, one of the worst hitting pitchers of all time, injured his arm after getting a hit in August 1964. He banged his elbow while diving back to the bag to avoid a pick-off. When the injury worsened, the team doctor diagnosed arthritis and said Koufax might do severe damage to his arm if he continued to pitch.

He did, though, for two more years, until he called it quits, saying, "I've got a lot of years to live after baseball. And I'd like to live them with the complete use of my body."

He was 30 years old and at the top of his game. He left it to baseball fans to imagine what his numbers would have been had his career run its natural course.

More numbers

Koufax was the first major league pitcher to throw four no-hitters. His last one, in September 1965, was a perfect game. He twice struck out 18 batters in a game. He was the league MVP in 1963, and in 1963 and 1965 he was the MVP of the World Series. His earned run average in World Series play was .95, first all-time among starting pitchers. His .655 winning percentage is 10th all-time. He was an all-star six times. He was the youngest man ever elected to the Hall of Fame, entering the Hall when many players older than him were still active.

Throwing Strikes

At his peak, he simply overwhelmed hitters with a virtually unhittable fastball and curve, while showing terrific control. In an era when the likes of Whitey Ford, Warren Spahn, Bob Gibson, and Juan Marichal were at their peaks, Koufax was the one who captured three Cy Young Awards as the best pitcher, not just in the league but in the game.

Throwing Balls

He was only at his peak for six years. Other pitchers had longer periods of greatness.

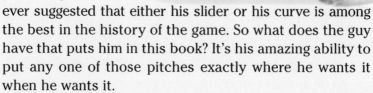

Gregory Alan Maddux (Greg)

b. April 14, 1966, San Angelo, Texas
Career: 1986–
Right-handed

Greg Maddux doesn't own an over-powering fastball, and no one has ever suggested that either his slider or his curve is among the best in the history of the game. So what does the guy have that puts him in this book? It's his amazing ability to put any one of those pitches exactly where he wants it when he wants it.

Actually, there is one other weapon Maddux has that few pitchers can equal—an amazing brain. Maddux not only looks like a college professor, he thinks like one. Most people keep charts on hitters. Maddux does much more. He records not only how every hitter does against him but how he reacts on every count and to every pitch.

"He's the most remarkable pitcher I've ever seen," said Yankee manager Joe Torre after Maddux shut out the Bombers in Game 2 of the 1996 World Series. "Every time you don't take a swing, it's a strike, and every time you do swing, it's a ball. It's like he knows whether the hitter is going to swing."

That's Greg Maddux: always thinking, always figuring out how to beat you. In 2002, at the age of 36, he went 16-6. His lifetime winning percentage is .642, including one season, 1995, when he was nearly unbeatable. That year, he went 19-2 with a 1.63 ERA. His winning percentage that season was .905. None of the other pitchers in this book ever had a season with a higher winning percentage than that.

But Maddux doesn't just beat hitters—he dominates them. Four times he has led the league in ERA. Since 1992, he has never been lower than eighth. Neither Pedro Martinez nor Roger Clemens can match that kind of consistency. Neither of them has ever won the Cy Young Award four years in a row, either.

Like many other modern-day players, Maddux learned to play baseball in Little League, but unlike most of the others, he had a big brother who would also go on to pitch in the majors. Mike, who is five years older than Greg, was a nice big brother and let Greg play with the big boys. It turned out to be a big boost to Greg's game, because it made him so much better than the boys his own age.

In Little League, he learned that control was more important than velocity. He was taught how to throw a variety of off-speed pitches and he learned how to make his fast-ball dip and tail. He also learned how to throw a change up. He was already so far ahead of other players his age that when he was 12 years old, other coaches refused to play his team when he was on the mound.

He was signed by the Cubs after he graduated from high school in 1984. By 1986, he was in the majors. He was so young looking that when he arrived in the Cubs dugout for the first time in 1986, his manager, Gene Michael, thought he was the bat boy!

It didn't take long for everyone who saw him to know exactly who and what he was. "That kid is a very tough pitcher," said opposing manager Whitey Herzog. "He knows what he's doing. He's going to win a lot of games."

Was Herzog ever right. In 1988, Maddux made his first all-star team and finished the season with an 18-8 record. Since then, he has always won at least 15 games a season. Maddux credits much of his success to hard work and preparation.

"I watch tapes of hitters all the time," he says. "When you go into a game with a certain plan and you execute it and it works, you walk away feeling like you've won, even if you didn't win the game. Stuff like that is what pitching is all about. Pitching is the art of messing up a hitter's timing, of outguessing the hitter."

Maddux's incredible numbers reflect all that hard work both on and off the mound. His 2.83 lifetime ERA is third among active players, behind Pedro Martinez and John Franco. Franco is a lifetime reliever, and Martinez has pitched seven fewer seasons than Maddux has.

His control has always been his strength. He has led the league in fewest walks per nine innings five times. Martinez never has. Is he the best in the game today? Randy Johnson thinks so. "I can still learn a lot from him by how he sets up hitters and his feel for the game," Johnson told an interviewer. "Without a doubt, Greg is probably the best pitcher to play in the last seven or eight years in the major leagues."

That's a pretty big vote right there.

More Numbers

He has led the league in wins three times to Martinez's one. He has led the league in shutouts five times. A terrific fielder, Maddux has won 12 Gold Glove Awards. He has led the league in complete games three times. He is an eight-time all-star.

Throwing Strikes

There may be no better finesse pitcher in the game today. At 36, he is as effective as he was at 26. The Atlanta Braves have been in the postseason every year since 1991 (they probably would have qualified in 1994, but the play-offs were canceled because of a players' strike), and Maddux has been a big reason for that success.

Throwing Balls

He doesn't have a great postseason record. In the World Series, he is 2-3. Overall, he is 11-13 in postseason play.

Juan Antonio Marichal

b. October 20, 1937, Laguna Verde,
   Dominican Republic
Career: 1960–1975
Record: 243-142
Right-handed

Juan Marichal had a pitching style they would never teach you in Little League. At the start of his windup, he would rear back, kick his left foot high in the air, thrust his glove hand forward while reaching back with his right hand, far enough to almost touch the dirt on the mound. Then he would shift his body forward and whip a slider, curve, screwball, or fastball to the plate from any one of a seemingly endless variety of angles and speeds. Throwing overhand, underhand, and sidearm, he confused hitters in the 1960s like no other pitcher in the league.

Marichal's high kick was effective because it kept hitters from seeing the ball as it left his hand. He was a 20-game winner six times, including four straight years, from 1963 to 1966. Twice he led the league in wins and he was a nine-time all-star. His chief rival at the time, Sandy Koufax, had three 20-win seasons and was an all-star six times. Marichal's other great rival from that period was Bob Gibson of the St. Louis Cardinals. Gibson had five 20-win seasons. Marichal's lifetime earned run average shaded Gibson's, 2.89 to 2.91, but Marichal had a much higher winning percentage than Gibson, .631 to .591.

With that high leg kick, you would think he'd have trouble finding the plate. Nope. He walked only 709 batters in 3,069 innings, an average of about two hitters per nine innings. Koufax averaged 3.2 walks per nine innings over his career. Gibson walked 3.1 batters per game.

How did he develop such control? Marichal took the lessons of David and Goliath to heart—he used a slingshot!

"To me, a slingshot was almost a piece of baseball equipment," he said in 1967. "I would sling a rock against a tree, or throw a baseball against the same tree, and the two were very much the same to me."

Marichal was a star pitcher in a Dominican amateur league when he was signed by the Escogido Leones, who had a working agreement with the San Francisco Giants. He was 22 when he made his debut with the Giants in 1960, and what a debut it was! Pitching against the Phillies, he was perfect through seven innings and finished the game with a one-hit victory, striking out 12. Four years later, he and Koufax led the majors with 25 victories. That season, he no-hit the Houston Colt .45s on only 89 pitches and was also the winner in one of the most amazing pitching duels in baseball history. On July 2 at Candlestick Park, Marichal took the mound against another future Hall of Fame pitcher, the Braves' Warren Spahn. Through 15 innings, both pitchers tossed shutouts, until Willie Mays ended the game with a home run off Spahn in the 16th.

In 1965, Marichal won 22 games. Ten of those victories were complete-game shutouts. His 191 victories during the 1960s were the highest in the decade. Next was Gibson with 164.

As great as he was, Marichal's reputation was damaged severely by a single horrible incident. On August 22, 1965, he smashed a bat over the head of Dodgers' catcher Johnny Roseboro in the middle of a game.

There was bad blood to begin with between the two California rivals, who were both chasing a pennant. Marichal started the game by sending Maury Wills and Ron Fairly sprawling in the dirt with inside pitches.

Because Dodger pitcher Sandy Koufax refused to throw at hitters, Roseboro took it on himself to respond when Marichal came to the plate by whizzing his throws back to the mound right by Marichal's nose. Marichal turned and had a few words with Roseboro. When Roseboro took off his mask, Marichal slammed him over the head several times with his bat. It was the most violent incident on a baseball field in the game's history. Luckily, Roseboro was not hurt seriously, although he could have been killed. Marichal was fined and suspended for a week, but the incident dogged him for the rest of his career. Although he was one of the most dominant pitchers of his era, he was not selected for the Hall of Fame in his first year of eligibility, 1982. He was, however, elected in his second year with the help of some intense lobbying by another former player—an ex-Dodger named Johnny Roseboro.

More numbers

Marichal led the league in shutouts twice. He was a brilliant all-star performer, pitching 18 total innings in eight all-star games with a .50 ERA. He was the first Latin American pitcher to enter the Hall of Fame.

Throwing Strikes

With his unique pitching style, he dominated the 1960s longer than any other pitcher with six 20-win seasons and an ERA well under 3.00.

Throwing Balls

As great as he was, he never won a Cy Young Award.

Pedro Jaime Martinez

b. October 25, 1971, Manoguayabo,
    Dominican Republic
Career: 1992–
Right-handed

Pedro Martinez's family was so poor when he was growing up that they couldn't afford to buy him a baseball, so the future Cy Young winner learned his craft by pitching with some very interesting objects. Sometimes it was a rolled-up sock. Sometimes it was fruit; other times, a rock. "When my sisters came home from school, they'd find their dolls with no heads," Martinez recalled. "I would take anything that was round to play baseball. That's the passion I had."

Nearly every young boy growing up in the Dominican Republic has the same passion for the game. It's amazing when you think about it. Almost 10 percent of all major league players come from this small, poor, island nation. The Martinez family has two of those players, Pedro and his older brother Ramon, who starred for several years as a pitcher with the Dodgers.

Pedro is Ramon's little brother not only in terms of years but also in size. Ramon is 6 feet 4 inches tall and weighs over 200 pounds. Pedro is 5 feet 11 inches and weighs 180 pounds. Still, he can throw a fastball over 97 mph, as well as a devastating change up and sharp curve. What also makes him so tough is that he can pretty much put any pitch where he wants, and very often that's inside on a hitter. In fact, Martinez hit so many batters early in his career that he earned the nickname "Señor Plunk."

Martinez has always said he doesn't deliberately throw at hitters, but he's not afraid of them, either. That fearlessness and his declaring that the inside part of the plate is his turf are big parts of what makes him so tough to hit.

"He's similar to Juan Marichal—fearless and challenging," said Martinez's former manager Felipe Alou. "He's a young, skinny kid throwing ninety-five-mile-per-hour fastballs inside on the plate. Batters don't like that. You have to be tough. If you're small, you've got to be tougher."

Martinez may be slightly built, but there's nothing slight about his arm strength. Even as a high schooler, he amazed adults with his speed. Scouts for the Dodgers were checking out his older brother when they noticed the skinny teenager throwing the ball better than 80 mph. They signed him to a professional contract in 1988 when he was only 16 years old.

Martinez moved steadily up through the minor leagues. He made his major league debut in 1992. While he had an excellent season in 1993, going 10-5 with a 2.61 ERA, the Dodgers traded him to Montreal to fill a hole they had at second base.

Do you think they regret that deal? By 1997, Martinez was the best pitcher in baseball. He won 17 games for the Expos, a team that could barely hit major league pitching. That season, he held opposing hitters to an incredible .184 batting average. His 1.90 ERA led the league. He also struck out 305 hitters. After the season, he won his first of four Cy Young Awards. And while 17 games may not seem like a high win total, it is when you realize that the Expos as a team won only 78 games.

Martinez was just getting started. Since 1997, he has gone 104-32. That's a .765 won-lost percentage. Randy Johnson's won-lost percentage over the same period is .741. Lifetime, Martinez also tops Johnson, .707 to .679.

Martinez has kept opposing hitters to a lower batting average than Johnson, .205 to .212. His lifetime ERA is also lower, 2.62 to 3.06. Martinez has a higher winning percentage and lower ERA than both Roger Clemens and Greg Maddux. Hitters have higher averages against Clemens and Maddux as well.

No wonder David Segui once said, "If the Lord were a pitcher, he would pitch like Pedro."

Martinez has captured four ERA crowns in the last six years. He has also led the league in strikeouts three out of the last four years. He is the first pitcher ever to win the Cy Young Award unanimously in two consecutive years. That's domination.

More numbers

Although his won-lost percentage will certainly decline as he ages, right now Martinez is first all-time. Playing for the Expos in 1994, he threw nine perfect innings in a game against the Padres before surrendering a hit in the 10th inning.

Throwing Strikes

Of all active pitchers, he has the highest winning percentage and the lowest ERA, along with four Cy Young Awards.

Throwing Balls

Other pitchers have been more durable and have averaged more innings per season. It may still be too early to judge his career value. He has won 20 or more games only twice.

Christopher Mathewson
(Christy, Matty, Big Six)

b. August 12, 1880, Factoryville,
  Pennsylvania
d. October 7, 1925, Saranac Lake,
  New York
Career: 1900–1916
Record: 373-188
Right-handed

At the turn of the century, hotels routinely refused service to both baseball players and dogs. That was for good reason. Neither could be counted on to exhibit even basic manners (although dogs at least were kept on leashes). Then Christy Mathewson came along. Here was a ballplayer whose honesty was so respected that if there was a close play on the field, the umpires would sometimes ask him to make the call. No wonder he was the first great sports hero of the 20th century.

Mathewson stood for everything that was good. He was college educated. He lived a clean life and if he wasn't a total goody two shoes, he was a gentleman. He was also one terrific pitcher.

"There is no doubt that Matty was the greatest pitcher of all time," said Mathewson's longtime catcher Roger Bresnahan, who is also a Hall of Famer. "He was the perfect pitcher. He always pitched to the batter's weakness. He had all kinds of stuff, and he knew just where to use it."

Rube Marquard pitched with Mathewson on his way to his own Hall of Fame career. Near the end of his life, he was still amazed at how good Matty was.

"Sitting on the bench watching him pitch, I often forgot I was a ballplayer, a pitcher myself. I became a fan. That's how good he was," Marquard told Lawrence Ritter for Ritter's classic book on baseball, *The Glory of Their Times*. "I've seen every pitcher you can name for the last seventy years, but Matty was the only one who ever made me feel like a fan."

Mathewson combined an excellent fastball and curve with a deadly pitch he called "the fadeaway" or "fallaway" (more about that in a while), but what really made him so great was his control. Had home plate been the size of a pinhead, he still could have thrown strikes. That's not such an exaggeration. One day he was giving a talk at West Point about pitching when one of the supervisors said he couldn't believe that Matty had the kind of control he was claimed to have had, so they made a bet. A stationary catcher's mitt was set up at home plate. Matty had to throw 20 balls into the mitt, including three curve balls. Matty won.

In 1913, Mathewson set a major league record by allowing just .62 walks per nine innings. At one point, he threw 68 consecutive innings without allowing a free pass. "You could sit in a rocking chair and catch Matty," said another one of his catchers, Chief Meyers.

Matty developed his control at an early age, although perhaps not in the nicest way. Growing up on a farm in Pennsylvania, he spent a lot of time tossing stones at birds and animals. "I used to go out in the woods and throw at squirrels and blackbirds, and even sparrows; and many a bag full of game I got with stones," he wrote in his autobiography.

Mathewson attended Bucknell University, where he was nicknamed "Gun Boots," because he was one of the best kickers in the country. But he left school in 1899 to join a semipro baseball team in Taunton, Massachusetts. On the team was a veteran pitcher named Virgil Garvin. Garvin had once been a major leaguer, and now he was trying to develop a pitch that would get him back into the big leagues. That pitch was what is today called the screwball. It is thrown by twisting the thumb toward the body. Garvin taught Matty the pitch, and in no time he mastered it.

"Such a ball is calculated to deceive the greatest batter," Matty wrote. "He is deceived at the start as to the speed of the ball. As it rushes toward him it looks like a fast high ball; six feet from him, when it begins to drop, it has the appearance of a slow drop ball, and then as he swings it is traveling in two directions at once."

But because the pitch put a lot of strain on his arm (try doing it yourself and see how unnatural it feels) he would only throw it maybe 10 or 12 times a game or when he needed it as his out pitch. It was part of his technique of pitching only as hard as he needed to, then bearing down when it was necessary. He called this "pitching in a pinch," and nobody did it better than he did.

Matty moved on to Norfolk, where he was 20-2 by July 1900, and caught the eye of major league scouts for the Cincinnati Reds. He became a New York Giant only as a result of a shady deal. The owner of the Reds was about to buy the New York Giants. New York's Amos Rusie, who had once been one of the best pitchers in baseball, was just about through. The Reds' owner, John T. Brush, wanted a good pitcher for his new team, and he couldn't have cared less about the Reds, so he arranged it so the Reds would get Rusie from the Giants in exchange for Mathewson's contract. Rusie's sore arm didn't improve, and he retired. As for Mathewson—well, he took the base-ball world by storm.

It didn't start off that way. He went 0-3 for the Giants in 1900 and was sent back to Virginia. When he returned, one of the geniuses in the Giants' front office tried to convert him into a first baseman until manager John McGraw put a stop to that experiment. In 1901, his first full season, he won 20 games for New York. It was the first of 13 seasons in which he won 20 or more games, a National League record that would later be tied by Warren Spahn. Mathewson, though, had 12 consecutive seasons in which he won more than 20. The best Spahn did was six in a row.

Also, in four of his 20-win seasons, Mathewson won 30 or more games. The most Spahn ever won in a year was 23 games. Matty won 30, 33, and 31 from 1903 to 1906. Grover Cleveland Alexander is the only other modern-day pitcher to win 30 or more three years in a row.

Alexander and Mathewson are both third in lifetime wins with 373 behind Cy Young and Walter Johnson. But Mathewson's .665 winning percentage is the highest of the four and his 2.13 ERA (fifth all-time) is the lowest of the four.

He led the league in wins four times and in ERA five times. His 1908 marks are some of the most dominating of any pitcher in a single season. He went 37-11 and led the league in wins, ERA, games started, complete games, innings pitched, strikeouts, shutouts, and saves.

No pitcher ever had a greater World Series performance than Matty did in 1905 against the Philadelphia Athletics. He pitched three of the five games and won all three on shutouts. Matty's lifetime World Series won-lost record is a less glittering 5-5. But the record is deceptive. His lifetime World Series ERA is 1.15 (eighth all-time). In several of those games, he was victimized by bad fielding. Probably the worst was in the last game of the 1912 World Series against the Red Sox, when Matty pitched brilliantly against Smokey Joe Wood, who was then enjoying one of the best seasons of any pitcher in major league history. (For more on Wood, see page 176.) The Giants got a run in the tenth for a 2-1 lead and looked as if they were about to win the Series, but in the bottom of the tenth, Giants' fielders flubbed two easy pop-ups, giving the Sox a 3-2 win and virtually handing them the Series.

Matty had enormous stamina. He started 551 games in his career and finished 435 of them. In most of those games, he threw fewer than 100 pitches. He was also helped by a photographic memory that allowed him to memorize the strengths and weaknesses of nearly every opposing hitter in the league. He was an avid chess and checkers player and was known to play up to eight checkers games at the same time—and win all of them. He didn't like to lose at anything. That prompted the journalist Damon Runyon to write, "Mathewson pitched against Cincinnati yesterday. Another way of putting it is that Cincinnati lost a game of baseball. The first statement means the same as the second."

In 1918, he enlisted in the military to support America's efforts in World War I. While in training, he was exposed to poison gas. His lungs were seared, and he developed tuberculosis. He never enjoyed good health again. When he died in 1925, the entire country went into mourning for its first great baseball hero, who had become a genuine American hero.

More numbers

He set 51 pitching records, 37 of them in World Series play. He led the league in shutouts four times and in strikeouts five times. When he retired, his 2,502 strikeouts were first all-time. His 80 shutouts are third.

Throwing Strikes

He had four great pitches and threw them all with amazing control. He was a great winner who beat the best at their best. He is the only pitcher in major league history in the top 10 lifetime in both wins and ERA. Those who saw him were in awe. Connie Mack, who spent nearly 70 years in the majors, said of him, "Mathewson was the greatest pitcher who ever lived. He had knowledge, judgment, perfect control, and form. It was wonderful to watch him pitch when he wasn't pitching against you."

Throwing Balls

Pitching for great teams, he led the league in winning percentage only twice. Three times he gave up the most hits of any pitcher.

Joseph Jerome McGinnity (Joe, Iron Man)

b. March 19, 1871, Rock Island, Illinois
d. November 14, 1929, Brooklyn, New York
Career: 1899–1908
Record: 247-144
Right-handed

In one month in 1903, Joe McGinnity pitched and won both games of a doubleheader three times. That season, he also set a National League record for most innings pitched with 434. But that's not why they called him "Iron Man."

Nope, they called him Iron Man because that's what he was—an iron man.

Around the turn of the 20th century, players didn't earn enough money during the baseball season to support their families, so they all had winter jobs. Joe's was in his father-in-law's iron foundry.

But he might as well have been the other kind of iron man. Four times in his 10-year career, he led the league in innings pitched. He was first in appearances six times, including five years in a row, from 1903 to 1907.

The guy just had incredible stamina. For one thing, he was one of the most powerful men ever to play the game. He was so strong that he owned a bar back home in a rough-and-tumble area, but he never had to hire a bouncer. He did that job himself.

He also knew how to pace himself during a game. He knew just when to bear down and when to save his energy. But mostly, his great ability to go and go was due to his unusual underhand pitching motion. He came upon the idea after a few mediocre seasons of semipro ball. He found that it not only put very little strain on his arm, but it also suddenly made him a very difficult pitcher to hit—for anybody. The story goes that when John McGraw was managing the Baltimore Orioles in 1898, one of his scouts told him about a pitcher he had seen strike out 22 members of an all-girls team in Arkansas. McGraw supposedly said, "Get him for me. If he can strike out twenty-two girls, perhaps he can strike out two men. And I don't have any pitchers who can."

In his rookie season, McGinnity led the league with 28 wins. Just to prove it was no fluke, he led the league in wins his second season as well, going 29-9 for Brooklyn. (The Orioles had folded.) He also led the league in innings pitched.

But McGinnity was only getting started. After he signed on with McGraw's Giants in 1902, he really hit his stride, and for the next six years, he and Christy Mathewson became the best one-two punch in the league. McGinnity led the league in wins again in 1903, 1904, and 1906. That means he led the league in wins for fully half his career, a percentage that's better than any pitcher in major league history. It would be tough to find a pitcher who had a better season than Iron Joe enjoyed in 1904. He was 35-8 for a league-leading .814 winning percentage. He was also first in ERA, games, shutouts, and innings pitched. This was in addition to astonishing the baseball world by single-handedly winning three doubleheaders in one month.

McGinnity won 247 games in his 10-year career, which means he averaged nearly 25 wins a season. Walter Johnson averaged 20 wins a season. Mathewson averaged 22. Lefty Grove's average was just under 18 wins a season; Three Finger Brown's, 17.

Always conscious of pacing himself, McGinnity rarely aired the ball out. He said a more slowly thrown ball was tougher to hit. He called his bread-and-butter pitch a "raise ball" (he also referred to it as "Old Sal"), because coming out of his underhand delivery it rose as it crossed home plate.

"It is not necessary to use speed," he wrote in his 1908 book *How to Pitch*. "In fact, lack of speed with good control is far better, for it is one of the most difficult deliveries of all for the batter to gauge since he can see the ball floating to him all the way, and yet finds it almost out of the question to estimate its speed so that he can hit it effectively."

McGinnity was a key figure in what is probably the wildest and most controversial play of all time. The 1908 pennant race was one of the tightest in major league history. The Giants and the Cubs were neck and neck. On September 23, they faced off against each other at the Giants' home, the Polo Grounds. The score was 1-1 in the bottom of the ninth, when, with men on first and second, the Giants' Al Bridwell lined a pitch over second, scoring Moose McCormick from second base. When McCormick scored, the man on first, Fred Merkle, leaped joyfully into the air and then ran into the dugout without touching second. Although the rules stated that he should have touched second before running off the field, it was not strictly enforced at the time.

But the Cubs' second baseman was a crafty player named Johnny Evers. He knew that if he could retrieve the ball and tag second, Merkle would technically be out and the run wouldn't count. That was the plan, anyway. But in the wake of the victory, there was chaos on the field as the fans poured onto the grass to celebrate. Still, Evers desperately screamed for the Cubs' center fielder to throw him the ball.

That's where McGinnity figures into the story. McGinnity had been coaching on third. He saw what Evers was trying to do. He also saw where the ball was still lying in the outfield grass. He broke into a run and got to the ball first. With the Cubs' shortstop, Joe Tinker, climbing on his back, the tough right-hander picked the ball up and threw it as hard as he could into the stands.

That should have been the end of it, but it wasn't. Suddenly, another ball appeared. Evers grabbed it and notified the umpire that he was touching second. The umpire had no choice but to call Merkle out. Since the game couldn't be resumed without creating a riot among the fans, it was called a tie. The league decided to replay the game at the end of the season if the two teams ended in a tie for first. That's exactly what happened, and in the play-off game, Three Finger Brown outpitched Christy Mathewson for the pennant.

For the rest of his life, McGinnity swore that Evers cheated. "I don't know where Evers got that ball he used to claim the force-out," McGinnity said, "but it wasn't the ball that Bridwell hit, because I flung that one out of sight."

Actually, even though he didn't pitch, McGinnity almost figured in the outcome of the play-off game as well. Before the game, McGraw sent him over to the Cubs' dugout to start a fight with Chicago's star first baseman, Frank Chance. McGraw was hoping that either Chance would get thrown out of the game (McGinnity, too, but he wasn't playing, so McGraw didn't care), or since the game was being played at the Polo Grounds, the umpires would declare that the Cubs forfeited by fighting and creating a dangerous situation. It didn't work, as Chance didn't want to risk a forfeit or two black eyes, so he refused to fight the Iron Man.

That year turned out to be McGinnity's last with the Giants. He became a player-manager in the minors the following season, but as he reached an age when other players took to their rocking chairs, he simply refused to stop pitching. Over the next 17 years, he won nearly 200 games in the minors, until he finally retired at age 54. Now that really is an iron man.

More numbers

McGinnity was also a regular reliever—he led the league in relief wins four times and in saves three times.

Throwing Strikes

McGinnity may have been the toughest pitcher who ever took the mound. He was also a great winner who led the league in wins for half of his career. No other pitcher has accomplished that feat. He averaged nearly 25 wins a season—the highest average among 20th-century pitchers.

Throwing Balls

His major league career was not as long as those of other great pitchers.

Charles Augustus Nichols (Kid)

b. September 14, 1869, Madison, Wisconsin
d. April 11, 1953, Kansas City, Missouri
Career: 1890–1901, 1904–1906
Record: 361-208
Right-handed

Charley Nichols was barely shaving when he signed his first professional contract at the age of 17. When he took the mound, the hardened minor leaguers made fun of the teenager by calling him "Kid." But the Kid soon wiped the smiles from their faces with a fastball that whizzed by the plate before they could even think about taking the bats off their shoulders.

In the 1890s, baseball fans argued over who was faster, Nichols or Amos Rusie. They didn't have machines to measure speed in those days, so no one really knew the answer. All they knew was that those two pitchers had the best fastballs anyone had ever seen—or couldn't see.

Nichols grew up in Kansas City, where he earned such a huge reputation in the local amateur leagues that he nearly signed to play with the local National League team. In the end, the teams decided against it only because the Kid really *was* a kid at 16. He did become a pro, though, at 17, when he signed with Kansas City of the Western Association. In 1889, while pitching for Omaha, he enjoyed what may have been the finest season of any minor league pitcher in history. He went 39-8 with 368 strikeouts and a 1.77 ERA. Think he was ready for the majors?

Frank Selee, the manager of the Boston Beaneaters, thought so. Selee signed the Kid for the 1890 season. The 21-year-old with the overhand motion and the high heat rewarded his manager's faith by winning 27 games and leading the league with seven shutouts. The Kid won more than 30 games in seven of the next eight seasons. No pitcher of the 1890s, including Rusie, won more games than Nichols. Cy Young, who won more games than any other pitcher, also made his debut in the majors in 1890, when he was two years older than Nichols. In the 1890s, when both were at their best, Nichols had a better won-lost record than Young, 297-151 to 267-151 for Young. He also had a lower ERA, 2.97 to 3.10, and pitched 300 more innings.

Nichols was a real workhorse. He threw over 400 innings in each of his first five seasons and over 300 innings his next five. He averaged over 337 innings a season during his career. Compare that with Christy Mathewson, who averaged 281 in his 17 years. Today's stars don't even come close to that. In his first 17 years in the league, Greg Maddux averaged 221 innings a year.

"If a pitcher wins fifteen games a year, he is considered great," Nichols said a few years before he died. "We used to work forty or fifty games a season, and I used to pitch every other day. If we got a kink in the arm we would just keep on pitching until we worked it out. Nowadays, they rush a pitcher off to the hospital."

Nichols said he never had a sore arm. He credited that to regular massage and his smooth overhand motion, which put very little stress on his arm. He said he also owed his success to his policy of sticking with basic pitches: fastball, curve, and change—although his out pitch was a rising fastball that he called a "jump ball."

"These young pitchers try too much fancy stuff and ruin their arms," he said. "I pitched with a straight overhand motion and never had much trouble."

He certainly didn't. He completed 95 percent of the games he started. His 533 complete games are fourth all-time. His

361 wins are tied with Pud Galvin for sixth place. That places him two behind Warren Spahn, who pitched six more years than Nichols did. But Nichols had a higher winning percentage than Spahn, .634 to .597. Young's winning percentage was .618; Rusie's, .586.

Baseball historians often say that 19th-century pitchers won more games and pitched more innings because they could afford to coast during games. The reason for that, they say, is that the dead ball made it unlikely they would give up long home runs. But Nichols threw hard for nine innings. He felt that was an important reason for his success. "In a game, a man should never let up on his speed in order to get the ball over," he said, "for if he does, a good hammering is generally the result."

Nichols was a winner when it counted. During his 12 years with Boston, the team won five pennants. Nichols led a pitching staff that most people said was the best of the decade. The rest of the team, with Hall of Famers Hugh Duffy, King Kelly, and Sliding Billy Hamilton, was pretty good, too. They were the Yankees before there were Yankees.

Nichols played a huge role in the team's success. In 1897, the Beaneaters went nose to nose nearly the entire season with the bad-boy Baltimore Orioles, a team that was notorious for its dirty play. From May until October, no more than two games ever separated the teams. It may have been the most exciting pennant race in baseball history. In late September, with the league championship on the line, Nichols beat the O's twice, and Boston went on to win the pennant by a single game.

Nichols led the league with 31 wins against only 11 losses in 1897 for a phenomenal .738 winning percentage. He also led the league in games and innings pitched and when he wasn't starting, he worked out of the bull pen. He even led the league in saves! As Nichols might say, "I kid you not."

More numbers

Nichols led the league in wins three seasons in a row, from 1896 to 1898. He had seven 30-win seasons and was only 30 when he won his 300th game. No other pitcher has ever won 300 that young. He is 11th all-time in innings pitched with 5,070, and fourth in complete games with 531. Although he was a power pitcher, he also had great control, walking slightly more than two batters a game.

Throwing Strikes

He was the dominant pitcher of his decade, a consistent winner, who led his team to five pennants.

Throwing Balls

Despite his great speed, he never led the league in strike-outs, and his 2.95 ERA was higher than those of other great pitchers of his era.

Leroy Robert Paige (Satchel)

b. July 7, 1906, Mobile, Alabama
d. June 8, 1982, Kansas City, Missouri
Career: 1948–1949, 1951–1953, 1965
Record: 28-31
Right-handed

On September 25, 1965, Satchel Paige took the mound for the Kansas City Athletics to face the Boston Red Sox. Pitching just three innings, he allowed no runs and only a single hit. An O.K. workout, nothing so special—except when you consider that Paige was 59 years old at the time.

In his five major league seasons, he had a 28-31 record with a 3.29 ERA, so why did Hall of Famers like Dizzy Dean and Joe DiMaggio consider him among the best pitchers who ever lived? Because he was. But because he was black and played at a time when minorities were barred from organized baseball, he was unable to prove it.

Satch spent most of his career playing for different teams in the Negro Leagues. Those leagues weren't always leagues in the sense that they played formal schedules against set teams. The Negro Leagues were often haphazardly organized. Players frequently jumped from one team to another. Some teams played set schedules only part of the year and barnstormed the rest, playing anyone from local amateur and semipro teams to squads made up of big leaguers looking to pick up extra bucks in the off-season. Because that was the case, you can't compare any of Satch's lifetime statistics with those of other major leaguers.

That means judgments must be made on the best possible evidence, such as eyewitness accounts and individual game reports, as well as some season statistics. That's a tragedy, because we will never know the full extent of Paige's brilliance. Still, as another Negro League star, Buck O'Neill, said at Paige's funeral, "Don't feel sorry for Satch or for the old men of the Negro Leagues. I feel sorry for your fathers and your mothers, because they didn't get to see us play."

What a loss for everyone. Here was a man who for more than 30 years could throw a baseball past anyone and with such accuracy that he could literally hit a nailhead from 60 feet away, and he didn't get the chance to show his great skills to most Americans until he was a 42-year-old rookie for the Cleveland Indians in 1948. Yet, after that heartwarming season, he was named Rookie of the Year. What he would have accomplished had he been able to pitch in the majors during his prime, we can only guess. In a sense, though, the racism that barred Paige and so many others from receiving the attention and rewards they deserved injured whites as well. For example, could Walter Johnson ever claim to be the best when he didn't have to face the likes of Oscar Charleston or Buck Leonard and others? Perhaps Johnson would have over-whelmed them with his great speed, but we'll never know.

Paige not only had great speed, but his control was phenomenal as well. Bill Veeck, who brought Paige to the Indians in 1948, saw Paige dramatically demonstrate his ability to put the ball literally on the head of a nail.

"He'd set up a one-by-two plank behind home plate and stick four ten-penny nails into it," Veeck recalled in his entertaining autobiography, *Veeck as in Wreck*. "Then he'd drive the nails into the board by pitching from the mound, and he never had to take more than ten pitches. That's control, man."

Paige came upon his incredible control naturally. Growing up in Mobile, Alabama, he would use rocks when he and his friends would go hunting—they would use BB guns. "He'd hit a bird flyin' in the air—bang, right in the head, and it'd fall out of the sky," one of his childhood friends told Paige's biographer, Mark Ribowsky. "He threw real straight, on a line. Nobody could throw like that."

It was around that time that he earned his nickname. Paige came from a poor family. To earn a little money, he and his friends would go down to the train station and offer to carry the bags of passengers for tips. Occasionally, Paige wouldn't return the person's bag. Instead, he'd take off with it. Once, a friend saw him running down the street with a satchel under his arm and an angry man only steps behind him.

"All those years he said he got the name 'cause he carried satchels. Hell no—it's 'cause he stole 'em," a friend recalled.

He wasn't a very good thief. When he tried to steal some jewelry, he was caught and sent to reform school. He spent five and half years there, but that's where he learned to pitch. When he got out, he joined his first professional team, the Chattanooga Black Look Outs, for $50 a month. Over the next 20 years, he played with nearly a dozen pro and semipro teams. They'd travel in old jalopies and worn-out buses (but occasionally in fancy railroad cars) to wherever they could find a game. Paige would pitch more than a hundred games a year, and he'd win most of them. At times he'd get bored with winning, so just to make it interesting, he'd deliberately walk two or three hitters and then see if he could strike the side out. Most of the time he did.

Paige led the Kansas City Monarchs to four consecutive Negro American League pennants. In 1942, he won three games in the Negro American League World Series against the powerful Homestead Grays.

Paige was 6 feet 4 inches tall, and his hands were so large that the ball looked like a pea when he threw it. Most of the time, he'd use a high-kicking delivery so that the ball was even harder to follow, but he had a whole host of deliveries, each designed to confuse hitters. He'd throw a straight fastball that he liked to call his "bee ball." Then he'd grip the ball across the seams and throw his "jump ball," which rose as it crossed the plate.

He also threw what he called his "hesitation pitch," where he would stop in midmotion just before delivering a tantalizing slow ball. That pitch was so effective, it was banned when he tried to use it in the major leagues.

"You knew what he was gonna throw you. You just couldn't hit it. It came in down here, but it wound up here," recalled Buck Leonard.

Throughout his career, Paige pitched in exhibition games against white teams. In the 1930s, he toured with Dizzy Dean and beat him regularly. Although he was a white Southerner, Dean had no trouble acknowledging Paige's enormous talent. "Why, if Satch and I were on the same ball club, we'd have the pennant clinched by the fourth of July, and we could go fishing until the World Series," he said.

Dean's teams were mostly filled with semipro players, but Satch also pitched against major league all-star teams. In 1936, he defeated a team featuring a young Joe DiMaggio. In four at-bats, DiMaggio managed only a scratch hit, and was happy to get that. "Now I know I can make it with the Yankees," he said after the game. "I finally got a hit off Ol' Satch." After he retired, DiMaggio said that Paige was the toughest right-hander he ever faced.

One year, Paige was set to tour against a group of major leaguers led by Hall of Fame slugger Jimmie Foxx. He beat them so easily in the first game, they canceled the rest of the tour. In 1946, he repeatedly outpitched a group of all-stars led by Bob Feller. By then, he was 40 years old!

In 1947, Jackie Robinson made his debut with the Brooklyn Dodgers, breaking the ban on black ballplayers. Veeck (who was barred from buying the Phillies during World War II when he said he would sign Negro League stars) moved quickly to sign Larry Doby, making Doby the American League's first African American player. Next, he set his sights on Satch, although first he had to convince his manager, Lou Boudreau, who had no interest in a 42-year-old "rookie." Veeck brought Paige in for a tryout anyway. At first, Boudreau, who was hitting nearly .400 at the time, tried to hit against Paige, but he could barely make contact against him. Next, Boudreau picked up a catcher's glove and had Paige pitch to him. Paige threw about two dozen pitches so accurately that Boudreau hardly had to move his glove. Ever the showman, Paige stepped off the mound and approached home. He then took a handkerchief from his pocket, folded it and placed it on a corner of the plate. He then went back to the mound and threw nine of his next ten pitches over the handkerchief. Boudreau had seen enough. "Don't let him get away, Bill. We can use him," he told Veeck.

Though so-called experts claimed that Veeck was making a mockery of the game by signing such an old man, Paige proved them wrong, going 6-1 with a 2.48 ERA and winning several key games down the stretch to help lead the Indians to the pennant.

Of course at 42, he was no longer throwing 100 mph. It was more like 95 mph mixed with a lot of trickery. When he didn't have his old smoke, he'd use an old-fashioned windmill windup or waggle the fingers of his glove, delaying his motion to make the hitters become overanxious. Then they'd swing early and miss.

133

"I uses more psychiatry than I used to," Paige told an interviewer. "I stares at them, slaps some rosin around and by the time I lets go, those batters' legs starts to wobble."

Asked whether he ever threw a spitter, Paige replied, "I ain't never thrown an illegal pitch. The trouble is, once in a while I tosses one that ain't been seen by this generation."

When Veeck sold the Indians and purchased the St. Louis Browns, he took Paige with him. In 1952, the 46-year-old Paige won 12 games for the lowly Browns. Veeck sold the Browns after the 1953 season, and the new management released Paige. But Paige's pitching days weren't over yet—far from it. He joined the Miami Marlins of the International League and went 11-4 with a 1.86 ERA for them in 1956, when he was 50 years old. In 1961, he pitched for another Triple-A club, the Portland Beavers of the Pacific Coast League. He worked 25 innings for the Beavers, fanning 19 hitters and giving up eight runs for a 2.88 ERA.

It seemed as if he would pitch forever. In the early 1950s, a *Time* magazine writer interviewed Paige and set down what he called "Satchel Paige's Prescription for a Long Life." Those six rules have since been widely quoted. Here they are:

1. Avoid fried meats, which angry up the blood.
2. If your stomach disputes you, lie down and pacify it with your cool thoughts.
3. Keep the juices flowing by jangling around gently as you move.
4. Go very lightly on the vices, such as carrying on in society. The social ramble ain't restful.
5. Avoid running at all times.
6. Don't look back. Something might be gaining on you.

It still sounds like pretty good advice.

Throwing Strikes

He may have had the most overpowering fastball in history, and perhaps no one ever combined such great speed and such amazing control. In contest after contest, he dominated not only Negro Leaguers but major leaguers as well.

Throwing Balls

He never had a real chance to prove his brilliance.

James Alvin Palmer (Jim, Cakes)

b. October 15, 1945, New York, New York
Career: 1965–1967, 1969–1984
Record: 268-152
Right-handed

Two years after Jim Palmer starred in the 1966 World Series, there wasn't a team in baseball that wanted him. At 23 years of age, with arm, shoulder, and back problems, he was over the hill. Not even the expansion Seattle Pilots and Kansas City Royals felt he was worth a chance.

Reluctantly, the Orioles kept him. After he had arm surgery, they sent him to the instructional league to work his way back into shape. The decision paid off—big time. In 1969, Palmer had a 16-4 record for the Orioles, leading the league with a .800 winning percentage. In 1970, he won 20 games for the first of eight times (in nine years), becoming the American League's best pitcher of the 1970s.

Palmer did it by pitching through the pain. He never really recovered from the torn rotator cuff in his shoulder that he suffered as a 20-year-old. In the days before arthroscopic surgery, a rotator-cuff injury was a one-way ticket to retirement. But Palmer went on to win 268 games. It makes you wonder how good he would have been if he hadn't been hurting.

"Pain was pretty much a part of my pitching career for the last fifteen or eighteen years," he said. "I was accused of not wanting to pitch with pain, but I pitched 4,000 innings, and probably 3,600 of those were after I tore my rotator cuff, so I had pain all the time."

One of the people who didn't believe it was his manager, Earl Weaver. The two had a stormy relationship, to say the least.

"I have more fights with Jim Palmer than with my wife," wrote Weaver in a book called *High Inside*. "The Chinese tell time by the 'Year of the Horse' or the 'Year of the Dragon.' I tell time by the 'Year of the Back,' the 'Year of the Elbow.' Every time Palmer reads about a new ailment, he seems to get it. This year it's the 'Year of the Ulnar Nerve.' Someone once asked me if I had any physical incapacities of my own. Know what I answered? 'Sure I do,' I said. 'One big one: Jim Palmer.'"

He may have been a pain in the butt to his manager, but he was a good pain in the butt. After 1969, any team would have been glad to take him off the Orioles' hands (or wings), but Palmer spent his entire career in Baltimore. And Palmer has a point when he said he pitched through pain. Four times he led the league in innings pitched and twice he led in games started.

Palmer was an orphan who never knew his real parents. He was raised in New York by a couple named Moe and Polly Wiesen. When Wiesen died suddenly of a heart attack, Jim and his mother moved to California, where she married an actor named Max Palmer.

Jim played only one year of minor league ball before the Orioles brought him up to the big leagues in 1965, when he was 19 years old. The next year, the Orioles won the World Series, beating the Dodgers in four straight. Palmer won Game 2, shutting out L.A. on four hits. (He defeated Sandy Koufax, who was pitching the final game of his career.)

His motion featured a high leg kick and a smooth delivery that was called pure poetry. "Jim had one of the most beautiful deliveries I've ever seen," said Ray Miller, his pitching coach. "It was almost like watching a ballet."

But it was the package that came with the delivery that made Palmer so great. He arrived in the majors with a terrific fastball, but it was the way he used it that made it so effective. "My first roommate was Robin Roberts," Palmer said. "Roberts told me that the best pitch was the high fastball, and I ought to be smart enough to throw it. He said, 'To succeed as a pitcher you can't be afraid to fail. You put yourself out there in the center of the diamond, and all the eyes are on you. You're supposed to be in control. You have to know what it takes to win.' Now, I'm a firm believer in that."

After his injury, Palmer lost something on his fastball, so he learned to mix it with an excellent change up and a curve ball that could freeze hitters in their tracks.

Palmer's other great asset was his mind. He approached every game with a plan. "The night before a start, I tried to visualize how I would pitch to every batter," he said. "They say a good manager stays two innings ahead. I pitched the whole game in my head."

On the mound, he would regularly place his fielders in position before he pitched. They didn't seem to mind, because he won so often. He led the league in wins three years in a row, from 1975 to 1977. He was also a two-time ERA champ. Three times he was given the Cy Young Award as the best pitcher in the league.

Palmer, who ate pancakes before every game (the reason why he was nicknamed "Cakes"), was also very particular about the baseballs he used during a game. If a ball had even the smallest blemish or didn't feel right in his hand, he would send it back to the umpire. The umpires enjoyed testing Palmer. Many times, instead of putting a ball Palmer had rejected out of play, the umpire would put it in his bag and toss it back into play several innings later just to see if Palmer would reject it again. Nearly every time he did. This was a man who knew what he wanted out there.

More numbers

Palmer was terrific when it mattered most. In league championship play, he was 4-1 with a 1.96 ERA, which is sixth all-time. His five complete games and 46 strikeouts are first all-time. He is the only pitcher ever to win World Series games in three different decades. His lifetime World Series record is 4-2. His postseason ERA of 2.74 is the lowest of any American League pitcher since the introduction of the lively ball. His 186 wins in the 1970s led all pitchers.

Throwing Strikes

Eight 20-win seasons in nine years shows terrific consistency and greatness. Only two other American League pitchers had as many 20-win seasons as Palmer, but neither Walter Johnson nor Lefty Grove pitched in the postwar era, when arguments can be made that the quality of the game improved, especially with the addition of black baseball players. Palmer was at his best when the pressure was the greatest.

Throwing Balls

He had many great seasons, but other pitchers had years that were better than Palmer's best.

Edward Stewart Plank (Gettysburg Eddie)

b. August 31, 1875, Gettysburg, Pennsylvania
d. February 24, 1926, Gettysburg, Pennsylvania
Career: 1901–1917
Record: 326-194
Left-handed

Eddie Plank drove hitters crazy. He would get the signal from the catcher, then he'd fuss with his shoes, then he'd hitch up his pants, then he'd paw at the dirt, then he'd stare at first, then he'd stare at third, then he'd stare at some fellow in a straw hat sitting 30 rows behind first, then he'd stare at the catcher again, probably because he'd forgotten what pitch he was supposed to throw, and then maybe he'd think about throwing the ball.

By then the batter was so eager to get on with it that he'd swing at anything.

So Plank would oblige with a lousy pitch that the batter would pop up. Then he'd move on to the next sucker.

People used to say that commuters didn't like going to the ballpark on the days that Plank pitched because they knew they were going to miss the train home. But Plank worked the routine so well that he won 326 games over 17 years.

What Plank was great at was outsmarting hitters. He was a college guy, after all, one of the few in the league at that time. Plank went to Gettysburg College, right near the historic Civil War battlefield. In fact, after his playing days were over, Plank worked as a guide there, preferring to talk about old generals rather than old hitters.

One of the amazing things about Plank's career is that he never played organized baseball until he went to college and the coach suggested he try out for the team. When he graduated from college at the age of 25, he was signed by Connie Mack of the A's and sent right up to the big leagues. By the time his career was over, he was the winningest left-hander in major league history. He held that record until Warren Spahn passed him in 1962.

"Plank was not the fastest. He was not the trickiest and not the possessor of the best stuff. He was just the greatest," said Hall of Famer Eddie Collins.

Plank's technique was to mix his fastball, thrown with a three-quarters motion, with a sidearm curve that he called his "crossfire." He also had great control, averaging fewer than two walks a game. He threw 412 complete games, 15th all time and 30 more than Spahn.

He won 20 or more games five times in six seasons between 1902 and 1907. The year he didn't win 20 he won 19—and his 19-6 record that season gave him the best winning percentage (.760) in the league.

Against Plank, batters crossed home about as often as the country elected a new president. His 69 shutouts are fifth on the all-time list. Spahn is sixth with 63. Plank nearly doubled Lefty Grove's 35 career shutouts. His career ERA of 2.34 is 13th all-time, bettering Grove's 3.06 by a wide margin. In his last season, as a 42-year-old, his ERA was 1.79. He was also still winning games. He banked 21 for St. Louis of the Federal League when he was 40.

Plank said the reason he lasted so long was that he saved wear and tear on his arm. "Like most youngsters, I started out with the idea that I would have to put all my strength into every pitch," he said. "But I made a study of pitching, and soon discovered that if I went on in this manner I could not last long. I then saved my strength for the critical stages of the game and now I do not put any more on the ball than I have to."

He was so careful about his arm that he rarely threw to first base to hold a runner. Fortunately, batters didn't get to first on Plank that often.

When it came to World Series play, though, Plank was one of the original hard-luck pitchers. His record was 2-5 in World Series competition, but—get this—his lifetime ERA in the fall classic is 1.32, good enough for 10th all-time. The problem was the A's never hit for him. He lost twice to the Giants in the 1905 World Series, even though he surrendered only three runs in 17 innings. Both times the A's were shut out. In the 1911 World Series, he earned a little revenge against New York when he outdueled Hall of Famer Rube Marquard in Game 2. The A's faced the Giants again in 1913. This time, Plank gave up two runs in 19 innings, losing Game 2 to Christy Mathewson, but besting Matty 3-1 in Game 5 to give the A's the championship.

More Numbers

Plank was the first American League pitcher to win 300 games. His 326 victories are tenth all-time. He won 20 games eight times in his 17 years.

Throwing Strikes

One of the smartest pitchers ever to play the game, he is among the leaders in wins, shutouts, winning percentage, and ERA. He had a very long career and was still a big winner when he was 40 years old.

Throwing Balls

He led the league in important pitching categories only eight times.

Charles Gardner Radbourn
(Charley, Old Hoss)

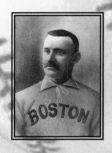

b. December 11, 1854, Rochester, New York
d. February 5, 1897, Bloomington, Illinois
Career: 1881–1891
Record: 311-194
Right-handed

The Holy Grail of all starting pitchers is a 20-win season. If you are a starter, you don't get into the Hall of Fame without having at least one. In 1884, Charles Radbourn had three.

That year Hoss won a major league record 60 games for the Providence Grays, carrying the team almost single-handedly to the world championship.

And to think it nearly didn't happen at all. Instead we might be talking about Jack Chesbro having the winningest single season in the history of the game.

Radbourn started the year off well, but during a game in July, he got so disgusted with the fielding behind him that he began lobbing the ball to the plate. He lost the game and afterward was suspended by manager Frank Bancroft. While Radbourn was still under suspension, the Grays' other starting pitcher, Frank Sweeny, jumped the team for another league.

The Grays were about to disband when Radbourn approached the manager with a deal: If the team would give him a raise to cover what he lost during his suspension, he would start every game for the rest of the season. Bancroft really had no choice and took Hoss up on his offer.

If ever a pitcher had a bionic arm, it was Radbourn. Of the 43 games that the Grays played from July 23 to

September 24, Radbourn started 40 and won 36. This was despite the fact that his arm ached so badly that after a game he couldn't raise his arm high enough to comb his hair. An assistant had to help him get dressed. His ERA for the year was a league-leading 1.38.

When the season came to a close, there was still more work for Radbourn, as the Grays challenged the New York Metropolitans for the world championship. It was a best-of-five series, and the Grays won it in three games. Guess who pitched all three?

Radbourn pitched 678 innings in 1884. Today, if a hurler works 200 innings a season, that's considered a lot. Even if you consider that pitchers didn't throw as hard back then as they do now, it's still an amazing total. At one point in the season, he won 18 straight games. He finished the season with a 60-12 record. The Grays, by the way, won 84 games.

Radbourn had to be a pretty tough guy, and he was. One of 18 children, he was a butcher before he played in the major leagues. When a reporter asked him if he got tired pitching every day, he had a ready answer: "Tired out of tossing a little five-ounce baseball for two hours? Man, I used to be a butcher. From four in the morning until eight at night I knocked down steers with a twenty-three-pound sledge."

Here's another indication of his toughness. Growing up in Illinois in the 1860s and 1870s, he had a drinking buddy by the name of Jesse James, who would become one of the most notorious bank robbers in American history.

Hoss was a wizard on the mound. He had a great fast-ball and a variety of curves. He also threw a knuckler, which was then called a "dry spitter." It was so effective that during one game the opposing team halted play, telling the umpire to examine the ball. "It's a crooked baseball. There's no honest ball could jump around like that."

The secret of Radbourn's success was his ability to put that dancing ball where he wanted it to go. "Any delivery without control is no delivery at all," he said.

He had an interesting way of teaching himself control. As a youngster, he would take whiskey bottles and put them on a tree stump, and then try to break them with fastballs and curve balls. It must have been effective. Over his career, Radbourn walked only 875 batters in 4,535 innings, which averages out to 1.7 walks per game. Compare that to a fine contemporary control pitcher such as Greg Maddux, who over his first 10 years averaged 2.6 walks per nine innings.

But unlike many great control pitchers, Radbourn also owned a terrific fastball with a lot of movement on it that leaped up at hitters. Early in his career, pitchers could still take a running start toward the plate as part of their windup, and Radbourn, who threw with a three-quarters underhand delivery, was said to throw the ball so hard that both his feet would leave the ground at the same time. Twice he led the league in strikeouts with that delivery, including 1884 when he struck out 441.

He was a National League star right from the beginning. His 25-11 record as a rookie led the league in winning percentage. The next season, he won 33 games and led the league with 49 victories in 1883, despite the Grays' winning only 58 games. Forty-nine victories were then a record number of wins in a season—a record he would, of course, break himself.

After that year, the rules for pitchers were changed. Now a pitcher was free to throw overhand. The only restriction was there was no more running start. A pitcher could take only one step before delivery. None of this was a problem for Radbourn. What was a problem for him was getting along with his teammates, and, as we saw, it nearly cost him his best season.

As it turned out, after 1884, Hoss became Old Hoss. His arm understandably tired out, and he was never the same pitcher, which means he was simply human. Pitching for an abysmal team, he won "only" 28 games the next year. In fact, he had four more seasons of 20 or more wins before he quit in 1891 with a 311-194 record. His 311 victories were the most by any pitcher when he retired. He was also first all-time in total games, starts, complete games, innings, and strikeouts. His lifetime earned run average was 2.67, which was second to Tim Keefe among the four 300-game winners of that era. Radbourn's average of 28 wins a year over his career, however, was highest among his rivals. Although a number of great pitchers boasted 30- and 40-win seasons in those years, nobody ever approached 60 wins, and it's safe to say nobody ever will again.

More Numbers

Radbourn averaged 412 innings over his 11 seasons. He led the league in winning percentage twice and in strikeouts twice.

Throwing Strikes

In 1884, he had maybe the most amazing season in baseball history. No one has ever approached the dominance, endurance, and mastery that Radbourn displayed that season.

Throwing Balls

After 1884, he never again had a totally dominating season. He lost more than 20 games in a season four times.

Amos Wilson Rusie
(The Hoosier Thunderbolt)

b. May 30, 1871, Mooresville, Indiana
d. December 6, 1942, Seattle, Washington
Career: 1889–1895, 1897–1898, 1901
Record: 245-174
Right-handed

Amos Rusie's fastball was so frightening that hitters would fake injuries on the days he was pitching so they wouldn't have to face him. They weren't just being cowards, either. Most of the time Rusie also had no idea where the ball was going—and remember, this was before batters wore helmets. Rusie once hit Hughie Jennings in the head with a pitch, knocking Jennings unconscious for four days.

Batters were so afraid to step in against him that the owners got together and moved the pitching mound back 10 feet where it is today—60 feet 6 inches from home. But Rusie's stuff was so good, the longer distance actually made him tougher to hit, because now he had enough room to snap off one of his crackling curve balls. The hitters were still so afraid of his fastball that the curve would leave them looking like statues, helplessly frozen while the ball dropped over the plate for strike three.

Rusie was a big Indiana farm boy, over 6 feet tall and more than 200 pounds. Word quickly spread about the boy with thunder in his right arm. He was still in his early teens when a state fair charged admission for people to come watch him launch baseballs through a wood fence.

Rusie began his semipro career as an outfielder. Then one day, the team's regular pitcher was knocked out of the game. A teammate suggested to the manager that he try Rusie on the mound. The manager took one glance at the kid's fastball, and Rusie's days of patrolling the outfield were over.

Rusie was still a teenager when he made his debut with the New York Giants in 1890. His 29 victories were the league's fourth best total. His 341 strikeouts were first by a huge margin. The second-place pitcher had 289. He was also in the top five in shutouts, innings, earned run average, games, and complete games. His terrific rookie season instantly made him the Big Apple's first sports celebrity. Beautiful actresses wanted to meet him. A drink was even named after him.

Of course, he had to live up to all that hype—and he did. The next season was the first of four in a row in which he won 30 or more games. He was also tops in strikeouts for the second straight year. Over his nine full seasons in the majors, he led the league in strikeouts five times. That's a better percentage than Walter Johnson, Bob Feller, Randy Johnson, Nolan Ryan, and Sandy Koufax. Rusie also led the league in shutouts in four of his nine seasons—again, an incredible percentage.

Rusie threw so hard that his catcher put a slab of lead over a sponge inside his glove to lessen the pain. Mickey Welch was one of the great pitchers of the 19th century. He lived long enough to see Rusie, Kid Nichols, Cy Young, and Walter Johnson pitch. It was Welch's opinion that Rusie was the fastest of the four. People were so amazed at his fastball that he wrote a book about it. The 25-cent paperback was called *Secrets of Amos Rusie, the World's Greatest Pitcher, How He Obtained His Incredible Speed on the Ball.* What a mouthful. Imagine going to a bookstore and asking for that one. But it was a huge seller in the 1890s.

Rusie struck out 1,934 batters in his career. That's not much when you compare it to Nolan Ryan's 5,714. But average it out per season and the two are much closer, with Rusie averaging 193 and Ryan 218. Ryan also won more games than Rusie, 324 to 245. But Rusie had a much better winning percentage, .585 to .526. And again, if you average out their victories per season, Rusie wins hands down, 27 to 12.

In 1894, the year he pitched the Giants to the championship, he led the league with 36 victories. He was also first in strikeouts, shutouts, and ERA.

It seemed as if nothing or no one could stop him, and no one could, except one man—the Giants' owner, Andrew Freedman, who makes George Steinbrenner look like Mr. Rogers. You would have thought that Freedman worshiped the ground Rusie walked on for all the people that he brought into the ballpark. But Freedman was a classic cheapskate who didn't like the fact that Rusie earned $2,500 a year. After the 1895 season, Freedman tried to dock Rusie $100 on the pretext that he refused to counsel one of the Giants' rookie pitchers. Then he fined him another $100, saying he missed a curfew. Rusie said he wasn't guilty of either charge, and since $200 represented a pretty good chunk of his salary, he said he wouldn't attend spring training in 1896 until Freedman rescinded the fines.

When Freedman refused, Rusie became the first star player to hold out. But he didn't stop there. He also threatened to take Freedman and the other owners to court over his loss of income and over the reserve clause, a baseball rule that prevented players from becoming free agents. That scared the dickens out of the other owners, because they knew full well that the reserve clause was illegal and wouldn't stand up in court. They begged Freedman to relent. When Freedman refused, the owners pooled their funds and paid Rusie $5,000 for the year. He made $2,500 just by sitting on his front porch.

The next spring, Freedman still wouldn't let his star put on a uniform. Then the fans got involved, and when they threatened to hang Freedman, he gave in. Rusie made a triumphant return, winning 28 games for the Giants in 1897.

Rusie started out brilliantly again in 1898, but while throwing to first base to keep a runner close, something popped in his shoulder. He continued to pitch, but the pain was so severe, he could only throw floating curve balls. After years of overwork, the muscles in his shoulder had given out. Rusie's thunderbolts were no more threatening than a gentle summer rain.

More numbers

Rusie was a workhorse. Three times he pitched 500 or more innings in a season. He averaged 418 innings a season over his career.

Throwing Strikes

His fastball was one of the wonders of the 19th century, but he was not only a strikeout artist, he was also a winner. He was so good, the rules were changed to give batters a chance against him. How many pitchers can you say that about?

Throwing Balls

He walked a lot of hitters, and other pitchers had higher winning percentages and longer careers.

Lynn Nolan Ryan (Nolan)

b. January 31, 1947, Refugio, Texas
Career: 1966–1993
Record: 324-292
Right-handed

When it comes to judging Nolan Ryan's place among baseball's greatest pitchers, you have to throw the usual statistics out the window. After all, the guy lost 292 games during his career, which is third all-time. He's also first in lifetime walks with 2,795. That's not something you brag about.

But on the other hand, there is the mind-blowing number of career strikeouts—5,714, breaking Walter Johnson's supposedly unbreakable mark by 2,200. Then there are the seven no-hitters to consider. Until Ryan came along, Sandy Koufax held the record with four, and few people thought that would ever be surpassed. But to nearly double it? That's like a pitcher raising Cy Young's record of 511 wins to 894, or George Bush breaking Franklin Roosevelt's record and being elected to seven terms!

Ryan owed his success to the Ryan Express, his amazing fastball, which was once timed at 100.9 mph on a day when Ryan said he wasn't throwing very well. Hitters would get very nervous when stepping in against him.

"Is there fear of Ryan? Sure, there's fear," said Hall of Fame third baseman Brooks Robinson. "There's an old baseball saying: 'Your heart might be in the batter's box, but your ass ain't.'"

The fact is that Ryan belongs here because he was capable of overwhelming even the best hitters in a way that few other pitchers ever could. It wasn't only with his fastball. He developed a very sharp curve and a change up coming off his fastball that some people called plain unfair.

And it's not as if his record is a poor one. He pitched 27 seasons in the majors, longer than any other pitcher in the game. He won 324 games, tying him for 12th all-time with Don Sutton. He did this while spending most of his best career pitching for very poor teams that didn't hit and didn't win. When Ryan was pitching for the Angels in the mid-1970s, the team ranged from awful to barely decent. Still, Ryan managed two 20-win seasons. Twice he rang up 19 victories. Had he been playing for a winner, there's no telling how many games he might have won.

Ryan grew up in Alvin, Texas, where he spent hours along the bayou throwing rocks at turtles and water moccasins. (Knowing his control problems, the reptiles probably weren't in too much danger.) Ryan later recalled that he strengthened his fingers and wrist tossing the *Houston Post* as a newspaper delivery boy. He pitched his first no-hitter for his Little League team. Although he could always throw a ball farther than anyone else, the great velocity didn't come to him until his sophomore year in high school. When it did arrive, it behaved like a runaway horse that refused to be tamed. Ryan never had any idea where the pitch was going. He was so wild that many times opposing players simply refused to bat against him for fear of being maimed.

One day in 1963, a scout for the New York Mets named Red Murff happened to be in the area and decided to take in a local baseball tournament. Ryan was pitching that day, and the scout was mesmerized. "Has the best arm I've ever seen in my life," Murff wrote in his report. Ryan was then only a high-school sophomore. Murff was so impressed, he kept tabs on Ryan for three years. When Ryan graduated, Murff persuaded the Mets to draft Ryan and take a chance that one day he might develop control. He did, but it didn't happen until after the Mets had traded him to California. Finally, after seven years in the majors, Ryan learned to stop overthrowing and pitch from a more compact motion. He also developed his nasty curve ball with the Angels.

The results were astonishing. In 1973, he became only the second player in major league history to strike out more than 300 batters two years in a row. In 1974, he made it three straight. From 1972 to 1977, he passed the 300 mark five times. He would add a sixth 300-strikeout season in 1989, fanning 301 hitters when he was 42 years old and still throwing fastballs in the high 90s. From 1972 to 1979, he led the league in strikeouts in every year but one and he led the entire majors five times.

In 1973, he raised Sandy Koufax's season strikeout mark of 382 up a notch to 383. Ryan's record is all the more remarkable when you consider that 1973 was the first year of the designated hitter in the American League. Had pitchers been batting that year, Ryan would easily have had more than 400 strikeouts.

Ryan broke another of Koufax's marks in 1973 when he struck out 10 or more batters in a game 23 times. He led the league in strikeouts per game in seven out of eight years from 1972 to 1979.

Ryan threw two no-hitters in 1973. He then added an unbelievable five more during his career. And—get this— he had 12 one-hitters. "I've had nineteen games in my career when I allowed one hit or less," Ryan wrote in his autobiography, "and when I think how close I came to no-hitters, I wonder what the no-hit record might be but for one pitch or one bad break."

Jeff Torborg was the catcher for the Angels whom Ryan credited for turning his career around. When

Torborg was with the Dodgers, he caught Koufax. He was once asked who was the faster of the two.

"When you talk velocity, Nolan threw the hardest," Torborg answered. "Nolan threw it down the strike zone harder than any human being I ever saw." He then told a story about one pitch in 1973 that he would never forget. "Against the Red Sox in 1973, Nolan threw a pitch a little up and over my left shoulder. I reached up for it and Nolan's pitch tore a hole in the webbing of my glove and smacked against the backstop at Fenway Park. It was kind of a frightening sensation. I wondered what might have happened if that ball had been thrown down in front of me. Oh, man!"

Ryan truly was a marvel. In 1990, when he was 43 years old, he led the league in strikeouts for the fourth consecutive season. When Walter Johnson was 43, he had been retired for three years. Cy Young was still pitching at 43, but the last time Cyclone led the league in strikeouts, he was 34 years old. Ryan not only broke Johnson's long-standing lifetime strikeout record of 3,508, he demolished it.

Ryan said that hard work was the key to his success. He didn't smoke and drank only an occasional beer. He also put himself through a brutal conditioning regime of weightlifting, lots and lots of sit-ups, and hours on a stationary bike. After pitching his seventh no-hitter at the age of 44 in 1991, he patiently answered questions from reporters and then excused himself to ride the stationary bike for 45 minutes. When Ryan was asked the secret to his success and longevity, he had a quick response: "The secret is knowing that there is no secret. There is just raw talent refined by hard work and humility."

More numbers

When it was long thought to be impossible to reach 4,000 strikeouts in a career (you would have to average 200 strikeouts a year for 20 years), Ryan passed 5,000. He retired with 5,714. A player would have to average nearly 300 a year for 20 years to top that. Ryan had only two 20-win seasons, but that number is misleading. Take his 1987 season, when he played for a very poor Houston team. His won-lost record was 8-16, but he led the league with 270 strikeouts and—for those who think he was only a strikeout pitcher—with a 2.76 ERA. He led the league twice in ERA, 11 times in strikeouts, and three times in shutouts. His 61 shutouts are seventh all-time (tied with Tom Seaver).

Throwing strikes

Strikeouts are important for a pitcher, and if they are your basis for judging greatness, then Ryan is your king. But as his seven no-hitters attest, he was more than just a strikeout pitcher. Had he pitched for better teams, his won-lost record would certainly be more impressive than it is.

Throwing balls

He did lose a lot of ball games and he walked more hitters than any other pitcher.

George Thomas Seaver (Tom)

b. November 17, 1944, Fresno, California
Career: 1967–1986
Record: 311-205
Right-handed

There's an old saying that if you're handed lemons, you should make lemonade. In other words, if you're dealt a setback, try to figure out a way to make the best of it. Tom Seaver did that so well, he became a Hall of Fame pitcher.

George, as he was known then, was a Little League star as a 12-year-old in Fresno, California. He even pitched a perfect game. But as the other boys around him grew, George stayed kind of small. Soon, the bigger boys were smacking Seaver's fastball around as if it were just hanging on a string in front of them.

So George thought about it awhile and decided that if he couldn't overpower the hitters, he could outthink them. "I tried to pitch with my head," he said later. He began to study pitching the way a scholar looks at ancient texts. He analyzed how a pitcher should stand on the mound, how he should wind up and follow through. He studied which pitch should be thrown in which situation and how to throw those pitches. In time, he grew to over 6 feet tall and could blow his fastball by anyone, but by then he had also become one of the smartest pitchers ever to take to the mound.

"He was a pitcher who thought like a catcher," said Johnny Bench, who caught Seaver when the two played for the Reds. "I never knew a pitcher with such a knowledge of pitching. He could outthink the hitters. That's the difference that makes the great ones great."

Even before he made it in the big leagues, Seaver's minor league manager, Solly Hemus, was impressed with the youngster's thinking and maturity. "Tom Seaver has a thirty-five-year-old head on top of a twenty-one-year-old body," he said.

Seaver was already an excellent pitcher at the University of Southern California when he was drafted by the Braves. But when the Braves illegally signed him to a contract, the commissioner's office canceled the deal and allowed other teams to bid for Seaver's services. All the team names were put into a hat, and a winner was picked. Ironically, the winner was the team that had hardly won anything up until then—the New York Mets. The team's fortunes were about to be dramatically changed with the arrival of Tom Terrific.

When Seaver joined the Mets in 1967, they were still the same terrible team that only once finished as high as ninth. In his rookie season, he managed to set a team record by winning 16 games. With the Mets' team batting average of .238, he did it mostly on his own. He probably would have won 25 with the pennant-winning Cardinals.

Despite Seaver's efforts, the team finished 10th in 1967 and 9th in 1968. But then in 1969 one of the great miracles in baseball history occurred. With Seaver's 25 wins leading the way, the lowly Mets captured the pennant and went on to defeat the heavily favored Baltimore Orioles in five games to win the World Series. That was also the year that America put a man on the moon. More than 30 years later, people still disagree over which was the more amazing achievement.

That season, Seaver won the first of his three Cy Young Awards. It was also the second of nine straight seasons in which he struck out 200 or more batters, a major league record that still stands. In five of those nine seasons he led the league in strikeouts. Had he fanned only four more hitters in 1977, the streak would have reached 11 with his 226 strikeouts in 1978.

In a game against San Diego in 1970, Seaver accomplished one of the most remarkable feats in baseball history when he struck out the last 10 San Diego Padres in a row. That, too, remains a major league record.

Seaver had an excellent slider to go along with his fastball. He said in an interview once that when his control was on, he could pitch to an exact spot nine out of ten pitches. He must have been on often. From 1967 to 1978, his ERA surpassed 3.00 only once. That was in 1974, when he played despite an injured hip. His lifetime 2.86 ERA is among the lowest of all pitchers since the onset of the lively ball era in 1920.

Seaver's winning percentage of .603 is not the highest among pitchers of his era, but other pitchers, such as Juan Marichal and Jim Palmer, played for much better teams. Still, of the three, Seaver won the most games and the most ERA titles. Bob Gibson's teams were better than Seaver's, but Seaver won more games than Gibson and more ERA titles and had a better lifetime winning percentage.

Seaver made himself a winner with his arm and his head. He was also a real competitor who was willing to do what he had to do in order to succeed. "Some pitchers want to be the fastest. Some want to have the greatest season ever. I wanted to be the best ever," he said. "If that means throwing logs on the fireplace with my left hand, then do it. If it means coming to Florida and wearing a shirt so my arm doesn't get sunburned; if it means in the winter I eat cottage cheese instead of chocolate chip cookies, do that, too."

Being a student of the game, he understood the process of "pitching in the pinch," the same technique of bearing down only when necessary that had been mastered by Christy Mathewson more than a half century before. Seaver talked about it in his book, *The Art of Pitching.* He said the difference between winning and losing a game usually came down to three or four crucial outs. That means the game could turn on three or four pitches. "One of the greatest challenges of pitching is to recognize these critical situations and to rise to the occasion," he wrote. "You can train yourself to identify the outs that you must get, and within the bounds of sportsmanship, to go about getting them."

Seaver mastered the technique well. He lasted 20 years in the majors, winning 20 or more games in a season five times. It probably would have been six if not for the strike-shortened 1981 season, which ended in July. At the time of the walkout, Seaver's record was 14-2.

If Tom Seaver had been a car, he would have been a Rolls-Royce: He was big and strong and engineered with intelligence and craftmanship for a smooth ride, day in and day out. As his former manager Sparky Anderson once said, "My idea of managing is giving the ball to Tom Seaver and sitting down and watching him work."

More numbers

Seaver led the league in wins and winning percentage three times. He was a three-time ERA champion. His 3,640 strikeouts are fourth all-time. His 61 shutouts are seventh (tied with Nolan Ryan). He made 12 all-star teams.

Throwing Strikes

Seaver's numbers rank with the best of the post–World War II pitchers, even though he was handicapped most of his career by poor teams playing behind him. He was a strikeout pitcher who also had consistently low ERAs and high winning percentages.

Throwing Balls

Other pitchers won 20 games more often and had higher winning percentages.

Warren Edward Spahn

b. April 23, 1921, Buffalo, New York
Career: 1942, 1946–1965
Record: 363-245
Left-handed

Warren Spahn was bald and had a big nose, and with his easygoing manner seemed more like your friendly neighborhood mailman than a brave war hero and the winningest left-hander of all time.

But a hero he was. Many ballplayers who were drafted during World War II spent the war in the rear echelon, playing for their camp ball clubs. The only fighting they saw was when a couple of fellows had too much to drink on a Saturday night. Not Spahnie. He served his country on the front lines in Europe and was wounded at Remagen, Germany, in a battle so fierce and so important that Hollywood made a movie about it called *The Bridge at Remagen*.

Spahn not only had courage, he also had perspective. "After you've slept in frozen tank ruts every day, baseball is a breeze," he said.

He certainly made it seem that way. Pitching with a fluid overhand motion, this graceful athlete had a career that spanned more than 20 years. Over that period, he won more than 20 games 13 times. That equals the number of 20-win seasons that Jim Palmer and Tom Seaver had *combined*. Spahn had 23 victories in 1963, leading the league in complete games with 22. That's three more than Koufax, who won the MVP Award. Plus, Spahn was 42 at the time. When Koufax was 42, he was playing golf every day. Nolan Ryan was still pitching when he was 42; his record that season was 16-10, with six complete games.

Spahn won 363 games, which is fifth all-time, but—get this—because of his war service, he didn't win his first game until he was 25. Christy Mathewson, a lifetime 373-game winner, snatched his first victory at the age of 20. Walter Johnson, a 417-game winner, was 19 when he notched No. 1.

Spahn believed his late start actually helped his career. "People say that my absence from the major leagues may have cost me a chance to win 400 games, but I don't know about that. I matured a lot in three years and I think I was a lot better equipped to handle major league hitters at twenty-five than I was at twenty-two. Also, I pitched until I was forty-four. Maybe I wouldn't have been able to do that otherwise."

Spahn was named for the man who was president when he was born, Warren Gamaliel Harding. He grew up in Buffalo, New York, where he played in every local league. He received a scholarship to attend Cornell, but because the Depression was still going on, he decided instead to sign with the Braves for $80 a month. That was a good salary back then.

Spahn pitched in spring training for the Braves in 1942. His manager, Casey Stengel, ordered him to deliberately throw a pitch at Pee Wee Reese's head. Spahn knew that Reese had just returned from a head injury, so he refused. That afternoon, Stengel sent Spahn down to the minors, saying he had no guts.

Spahn spent the next 23 years (including his three years overseas in the army) proving Stengel wrong. In 1965, when he joined the awful New York Mets, then managed by Stengel, Spahn joked, "I'm the only one who played for Stengel before and after he was a genius."

When he returned from the war, Spahn quickly showed plenty of guts on the mound. In 1947, he won 21 games on the strength of a low fastball, sharp curve, and uncanny control. Spahn threw every pitch from the same overhead motion, but because of his high leg kick, batters had a difficult time picking up the ball. They had an even harder time after he added a screwball and a slider to his repertoire. Spahn's motion was so efficient, he never once had a sore arm. His 17 seasons of 245 or more innings are a National League record. He led the league in innings pitched four times.

Although he won "only" 15 games in 1948, he and the Braves' other great starter, Johnny Sain, led the team to the pennant. It's a measure of how good Spahn and Sain were that the team captured the pennant with basically just two good starting pitchers. It even inspired one of baseball's most well known bits of doggerel: "Spahn and Sain and pray for rain."

From 1949 through 1963, he failed to win 20 games only three times. Three times during that period he led the league in shutouts. Nine times he led the league in complete games, a major league record. His 382 lifetime complete games are a National League record for left-handers. The major league mark for lefties is Eddie Plank's 412; surely, Spahn would have topped that had he not lost three years to the military. While Cy Young completed nearly twice as many games as Spahn, he pitched during a time when pitchers remained in games no matter what. In fact, Young led the league in complete games only three times.

Spahn led the league in wins eight times, another major league record. At one point, he led the league five seasons in a row. He did it not only with his athleticism but also with his brain. "He makes my job easy," said the Braves' pitching coach, Whitlow Wyatt. "Every pitch he throws has an idea behind it."

After a game, Spahn could recount every pitch and where he had thrown it. Wyatt recalled talking to Spahn one day about a game 15 years earlier, when Wyatt was pitching and Spahn was hitting. "He reminded me that the first time I faced him I threw him a fastball, then a curve, then another fastball that he hit to the shortstop. He not only remembered the hitters, but the pitchers, too," Wyatt said.

The Hall of Fame hitter Stan Musial called Spahn "an artist with imagination." His former manager Chuck Dressen called him his "go-to-sleep pitcher." "I go to bed the night before Spahn pitches and get a good night's sleep," he explained.

Spahn's theory about pitching was simple. "Hitting is timing. Pitching is upsetting timing," he said.

He was upsetting the timing of hitters at an age when most pitchers had retired to their rocking chairs. He pitched his first no-hitter in 1960, when he was 39 years old, and just to prove it was no fluke, he pitched another the next season, five days after his 40th birthday.

Spahn loved baseball and loved competing. When he was released by the Giants after the 1965 season, he pitched in the minors for a couple of years. If it were up to him, he'd probably still be pitching, and as of this writing he's over 80 years old. "I didn't quit baseball," he said after his retirement. "Baseball retired me."

More numbers

Spahn was also an excellent hitter with 35 lifetime home runs, the National League record. His 750 appearances are 10th among starting pitchers. His 5,244 innings are eighth lifetime and first among left-handers. He had 382 complete games, first among post–World War I pitchers. He was the ERA leader three times. Spahn's 63 shutouts are sixth on the all-time list and first among pitchers of his era. His 665 starts established a National League record. He was named to the all-star team 14 times.

Throwing Strikes

He won more games than any left-hander and not only pitched for more than 20 years but dominated for 20 years. He holds many lifetime records and also led the league in 35 categories during his career.

Throwing Balls

He lost 245 games, and his winning percentage was lower than that of other pitchers.

Edward Augustine Walsh (Big Ed)

b. May 14, 1881, Plains, Pennsylvania
d. May 26, 1959, Pompano Beach, Florida
Career: 1904–1917
Record: 195-126
Right-handed

Ed Walsh was such a confident pitcher that one writer said he was the only person he knew "who could strut while he was standing still."

What gave Walsh such confidence was his ability to master the spitball. Many pitchers threw it, but few knew where it was headed. That, and not the fact that many people thought it was disgusting, was what actually led to it being banned after the 1920 season.

But we're getting ahead of our story. At 6 feet 1 inch tall, Walsh was a big guy in the olden days. (If he were playing today, he'd probably be called "Medium Ed.")

Ed wasn't just big in terms of height—he was strong, too. He earned his muscles the hard way, as a young boy working in the Pennsylvania coal mines. Walsh drove a mule in the mines. Later on in his baseball career when he was referred to as a workhorse, he knew probably better than anybody what that really meant.

Here's why they called him a workhorse. He led the league in appearances five times between 1907 and 1912. He was first in innings pitched four times. Cy Young led the league in innings pitched twice during his 22-year career. Warren Spahn was tops in innings pitched four times, but the total innings he pitched in those four years was 1,174. Walsh's total was 1,648.

The 1908 season was his best and one of the best ever for any pitcher. He pitched 464 innings, setting a record for a modern-day pitcher that will most likely never be broken. His 66 appearances set a record that stood for 56 years, until it was broken by a reliever. Walsh started nearly every other day. He went 40-15 in 1908. He was the last pitcher to win 40 in a season and he did it for a team that wasn't very good. The 40 games represented 45 percent of the White Sox's wins. That's the highest percentage of a team's victories in American League history.

It gets better. During one eight-day span, he pitched 41 innings. He pitched two games in a doubleheader, winning both while giving up only one run. In 1908, he also led in starts, complete games, shutouts, saves, and strikeouts.

Walsh wasn't always so dominant. He arrived in the majors with a decent fastball and a mediocre curve. Then his manager had him room with another pitcher, Elmer Stricklett. Stricklett turned out to be a great choice as a roommate, not because he didn't snore, but because he was willing to show Walsh how to throw the spitball. It took Walsh two years to learn how to control the pitch, but then he rode the wet one right into the Hall of Fame.

"That ball disintegrated on the way to the plate, and the catcher put it back together again," said Hall of Famer Sam Crawford about Walsh's spitball. "I swear, when it went past the plate it was just spit that went by."

Actually, Walsh didn't spit on the ball. Few pitchers did. That really would be gross. What he would do was chew on a piece of gum or a substance called slippery elm bark, which produced a steady stream of saliva. He would then wet his fingers and grip the ball with his index and middle fingers on top and his thumb underneath.

"Learning the release is the trick," Walsh explained. The theory behind it is that the wet spot on the ball prevents the fingers from gripping the ball tightly. When a pitcher lets the ball slip from his fingers, it speeds toward the plate without spinning. That allows it to ride the wind currents, dipping and diving in different directions, like a surfer on the waves off the southern California coast. That's why it's so hard to hit, because most of the time a batter has no idea where the ball is going. Neither do most pitchers, although Walsh said he could actually control its direction. If that was true, he was just about the only one.

But baseball can be a very cruel sport, and even Walsh was victimized by the very pitch that got him into the Hall of Fame. It happened, oddly enough, in what Walsh said was the best game he ever pitched. It's certainly a candidate for baseball's most dramatic pitching duel. On October 2, 1908, Walsh's White Sox took on Addie Joss and the Cleveland Indians, with both teams battling for the pennant. Walsh lost when Cleveland scored the only run in the game after one of his spitters broke so sharply that it got away from his catcher and actually broke his finger. Joss came away the winner of a perfect game, 1-0. But as it turned out, neither team won the pennant, as Detroit, led by a kid named Ty Cobb, took first place. The White Sox finished third, even though their batting average was second lowest in the league.

The next year, Walsh won only 15 games, but of those 15 wins, eight were shutouts. His ERA that season was 1.41, good enough for second in the league, and that was considered an off year! In 1910, he lowered his ERA to a league-leading 1.27, even though he lost 20 games that season. During the years he pitched for them, the White Sox batters were so pathetic that they were known as the "Hitless Wonders." Those ERA numbers make you think how many more 40-win seasons Walsh would have won if the Sox had been even an average hitting team.

The name of the game when you're a pitcher is keeping the opponent from scoring runs. At that, Walsh was the best. His lifetime ERA of 1.82 is not only the lowest of all major league pitchers, but he and Joss are the only pitchers under 2.00. Walsh's 1.82 is six one-hundredths of a point lower than Joss's 1.88. No one else is even within spitting distance.

More numbers:

Walsh led the league in strikeouts twice, ERA twice, and shutouts three times. The rubber-armed hurler was also the saves leader five times. He won more than 20 games in a season four times.

Throwing Strikes

No one gave up fewer runs per nine innings than Walsh. His 1908 season, when he won 40 games and lost only 15, ranks as one of the best ever.

Throwing Balls

He didn't win 200 games.

Denton True Young (Cy)

b. March 29, 1867, Gilmore, Ohio
d. November 4, 1955, Newcomerstown, Ohio
Career: 1890–1911
Record: 511-316
Right-handed

Who is the only player in major league history who was so great they named a major award for him?

If you said Harry Valuable, you would be wrong.

Is it any surprise that it's Cy Young?

The Cy Young Award is given to the best pitcher in the National and American Leagues. Roger Clemens has won it six times. Who knows how many times Cy Young would have won it during his career. Young pitched 22 years in the majors. He won more games than any other pitcher in major league history. That's a big one when you're deciding who was the best pitcher in the game. And it's not as though he eked his way into the top spot, either. He is nearly 100 games ahead of the second-place finisher, Walter Johnson. Grover Cleveland Alexander and Christy Mathewson, who are tied for third with 373, aren't even in the ballpark.

Young's first professional experience was with Canton in the Tri-State League. That's where he supposedly got his nickname. He was trying out for the team when his catcher got a look at Young's blazing fastball and pronounced it "as fast as a cyclone." Years later, Hall of Famer Tris Speaker said Young could bring it as fast as Walter Johnson and Bob Feller.

But he didn't have only a terrific fastball. He also threw a "drop ball," which was a big curve that fell off the table, a sidearm curve he called a "swerve," and—to top it off—a terrific change up that froze hitters who were trying to time his fastball. He pitched with four motions, and as if that wasn't confusing enough, he started them all with his back to the plate.

But it wasn't just the speed or the variety of pitches that made Young so overpowering—it was his ability to put his pitches wherever he wanted. No fastballer in history had Young's control. From 1893 to 1905, he led the league 13 times in fewest walks per game, an amazing record. Christy Mathewson, who didn't throw nearly as hard as Young did, led the league seven times. Walter Johnson did it twice. Kid Nichols did it once. Bob Feller, another fireballer from a later era, never did, and Amos Rusie, who could hardly hit a barn from 15 feet away, never did, either.

There was another reason for Young's success: a photographic memory. He could recall every hitter he faced, his strengths and weaknesses, and how he hit against him.

After Young went 15-15 for Canton, the team offered him around to the major leagues for $500 but couldn't find any takers until the Cleveland Spiders decided to gamble on him. You could say they enjoyed a pretty good payoff. After a 9-7 rookie season, he won 21 or more games for the next eight years. In three of those seasons, he won more than 30 games. In all, Young won 20 or more games 15 times, a major league record. What made it even more remarkable was that most of the teams he pitched for were pretty lousy. In 22 seasons he played for only two champions.

In 1901, Young moved over to the Boston Pilgrims of the newborn American League and became the junior circuit's first pitching superstar. He starred in the first modern-day World Series in 1903. Young started three games against the Pirates, who were led by the great Honus Wagner.

Young won two of them and had a 1.59 ERA to spark the Pilgrims' upset victory.

At 6 feet 2 inches and over 200 pounds, Young was a big country boy. He learned his trade by pitching oranges on his father's farm. But it wasn't all play. Young said the hard farm life was responsible for his long career. Every winter he would chop wood and do the heavy chores that needed to be done so he was already in pretty good shape when spring training rolled around.

"I worked hard all winter on my farm, from sunup to sundown, doing chores that not only were good for my legs, but also for my arms and back," he said. "Swinging an axe hardens the hands and builds up the shoulders and back. I needed only a dozen pitches to warm up for a ball game."

He must have known what he was doing. Young never once had a sore arm, even though he had 16 seasons in which he pitched 300 innings or more, a major league record that is unbelievable when you consider that modern-day workhorses such as Roger Clemens and Nolan Ryan don't pitch nearly that much.

He also owns the major league record for complete games (749) and innings pitched (7,356). In both cases, the second-place pitcher, Pud Galvin, isn't even close. In all, when he retired, Young had set some 93 pitching records—that, too, is a major league record. Young was either a leader or among the leaders in most of the important pitching categories. He led the American League in wins in each of its first three years of operation. During his career, he was a league leader 31 times, including seven times in shutouts.

But while all that farm work did wonders for his arm, apparently, it didn't include a lot of sit-ups. If you see pictures of Young late in his career, you'll see he acquired the same shape as Babe Ruth or your uncle whose only exercise is turning on TV and reaching into a box of jelly doughnuts. But it didn't hurt the Babe at the plate, and it clearly didn't hurt Young on the mound, either, until very late in his career when he had to retire—not because he couldn't pitch any more, but because opposing hitters were taking advantage of the fact that he was too fat to field bunts.

"I don't expect to see a second Cy Young," said Hall of Famer John McGraw, who hit against Young many times during his career. "Men who combine his talents of mind and arm are not born often."

Young enjoyed talking about the art of pitching. He even put together what he called "The Rules for Pitching Success." Here they are:

1. Pitchers, like poets, are born, not made.
2. Cultivate good habits: Let liquor severely alone, fight shy of cigarettes, and be moderate in indulgence of tobacco, coffee, and tea. A player should try to get along without any stimulants at all: Water, pure cool water, is good enough for any man.
3. A man who is not willing to work from dewy morn until weary eve should not think about becoming a pitcher.
4. Learn to be patient and cool. These traits can be cultivated.
5. Take the slumps that come your way. Ride over them, and look forward.
6. Until you can put the ball over the pan whenever you choose, you have not acquired the command necessary to make a first-class pitcher. Therefore, start in to acquire command.

With 511 wins to his name, a record that might never be broken, you have to figure he knew what he was talking about.

More numbers

Young also holds the major league record for career pitching starts with 815. He finished 750 of those games, another major league record. When he retired in 1911, he held the major league strikeout record with 2,803. He is fourth all-time in shutouts with 76. Consider this about his 511 wins: A pitcher can average 25 wins a year for 20 years and still not pass Young.

Throwing Strikes

He won more games and set more records than any other pitcher, all while pitching for poor teams. But he not only measures up against the best in terms of lifetime numbers, he was also dominating against his contemporaries.

Throwing Balls

He is first all-time in losses with 316.

Who's It Gonna Be?

You made it—congratulations!

Hey, did you skip Eddie Plank? I knew it. Go back and read about him. You can't decide who is the best until you read them all. We'll still be here when you're done.

O.K., now that you've read all 33, why not pare your selections down to a final five. Then make a list for and against each one. Try to weigh the different statistics and the other aspects of their careers. How important is it that a pitcher may or may not have won 300 games? Can a pitcher who won fewer than 200 games still be in the running as the best? How important are strikeouts? How important are complete games—especially if everyone was pitching complete games? How important is the number of times a pitcher led in a certain category, as opposed to the percentage of times in proportion to his career that he was the leader? In other words, if someone led the league in strikeouts seven times in a 24-year career, is that more impressive than another pitcher who led in strikeouts five times in a 10-year career? Which era had the toughest competition? Could Old Hoss Radbourn have won 60 games if he had pitched against the likes of Babe Ruth and

Murderers' Row? How would Pedro Martinez have fared in the Dead Ball Era? How would Lefty Grove do against today's competition? Here's another way to look at it: Is the best pitcher the one who was the most dominant in his era? If that's the case, who would that be? Or if you had to win one game, which of the pitchers on the list would you choose? How important is that in deciding who is best?

So ponder, and ponder some more. Make your own list of standards or questions that you think need to be answered before you can arrive at a decision. After you've made your choice, drop me a line. I'd love to know who you picked and why.

But wait. I'm not going to let you go so easily. Baseball historian Bill James has two categories for rating pitchers: lifetime value and peak value. This book is really about deciding who was the best over his entire career. But why not look at it the other way? So the question is: At his absolute highest peak in performance over a single season, which pitcher was the best? That means you can bring in other pitchers who aren't mentioned in the book. For example, there's Dutch Leonard, who holds the modern record for the lowest earned run average in a season with his 1.01, when he went 19-5 in 1914. You should also consider Jack Chesbro, who went 40-12 in 1904. More recently, there's Ron Guidry, who in 1978 went 25-3 for the Yankees. What about Smokey Joe Wood in 1912, the year he won 34 against five losses and bested Walter Johnson in baseball's version of the fight of the century? There's also Orel Hershiser's season in 1988, when he set the major league record with 59 consecutive scoreless innings and was unbeatable in the postseason. How do they measure up against the best seasons of the pitchers in this book: Old

Hoss Radbourn in 1884, Christy Mathewson in 1908, Walter Johnson in 1913, Dizzy Dean in 1934, or Steve Carlton in 1972. Was there any better pitcher than Bob Gibson in 1968? You decide.

Further Reading

The Autobiography of Baseball: The Inside Stories from the Stars Who Played the Game, by Joseph Wallace (New York: Harry N. Abrams, 1998). This is a beautiful book, filled with loads of great photographs. The stars discuss many aspects of the game, including how it was played, the techniques they used, and their lives as baseball players. If you enjoy playing baseball, there are lots of great tips from some of the best who ever played.

The Baseball Encyclopedia: The Complete and Definitive Record of Major League Baseball, Tenth Edition (New York: Macmillan, 1996). If there is a baseball Bible, this is it. I got nearly all the stats you've read in this book from the encyclopedia. It's an amazing compilation and great fun just to pick through for all sorts of wonderful statistics, history, and trivia about baseball. It's so heavy you might need a crane to pick it up, but it's worth every pound.

Baseball Extra: A Newspaper History of the Glorious Game from Its Beginnings to the Present, compiled by Eric Caren (Edison, N. J.: Castle Books, 2000). Boy, is this fun! This large book tells the history of baseball through reproductions of newspaper pages through the years. Here you can read the actual stories of most of the great moments in baseball history. Because entire pages are reproduced, a special bonus is the other news stories you can read from the world of sports and the real world as well.

Baseball's Hall of Fame: Cooperstown, Where the Legends of Baseball Live Forever, by Lowell Reidenbaugh (New York: Crescent, 1997). This book has a one- or two-page biography of every Hall of Famer, along with photos and statistics.

The Cultural Encyclopedia of Baseball, by Jonathan Fraser Light (Jefferson, N.C.: McFarland, 1997). I discovered this amazing book this year. It has thousands of entries on everything from A to Y (Henry Aaron to youth baseball) that's related to baseball. There are entries on baseball films, managers, the Hall of Fame—even a section on gum! Light has included tons of anecdotes, quotes, and statistics. What a job he has done! Each entry is a joy to read.

The Glory of Their Times: The Story of the Early Days of Baseball Told By the Men Who Played It, by Lawrence Ritter (New York: Morrow, 1984). As time goes by, this book just gets better and better. In the 1960s, Ritter taped the recollections of some of baseball's oldest retired players, and here they are talking about the game and its players around the turn of the 20th century up to World War II. If you really want to know what the game was like back then, this book is for you.

The Head Game: Baseball Seen from the Pitcher's Mound, by Roger Kahn (New York: Harcourt, 2000). This is a book that is devoted to the art and science of pitching, presented in the words and wisdom of some of the game's greatest twirlers.

The New Bill James Historical Baseball Abstract, by Bill James (New York: The Free Press, 2001). This guy is so good that he even gets his name in the title! This is another book that is just great fun to pick through. James has put together a wonderful look at baseball through the decades, with fascinating sections devoted to topics such as uniforms, the Negro Leagues, the best minor league team ever, and nicknames. Each decade also has a separate box with entries for the heaviest player, best baseball books, hardest throwing pitcher, ugliest player, "A Better Ballplayer Than a Human Being," and many more. Then there's the meat of the book, where he rates the top 100 players at each position, with comments and stories about each of them.

Total Baseball: The Official Encyclopedia of Major League Baseball, Seventh Edition, edited by John Thorn, Pete Palmer, and Michael Gershman (New York: Warner Books, 2001). This is a great companion volume of stats to *The Baseball Encyclopedia,* even though you will find the two often have different statistics for the same players. Like the *Encyclopedia,* it also has a lot of great articles and, like the *Encyclopedia,* you'll need a crane to lift it, but if you get this book, you will be reading it for years and forever learning something new.

Who Is Baseball's Greatest Hitter? by Jeff Kisseloff (New York: Henry Holt, 2001). I don't know who this guy thinks he is or if this book is any good, but he paid me a fortune to include it on this list.

Acknowledgments

If you think this book was a great idea, don't thank me, thank Marc Aronson of Carus Publishing who thought it up and was nice enough to ask me to do it.

When you write a book like this, there are a lot of people whose job it is to make sure you don't look like an idiot. They are called editors, and, fortunately for me, they put in a lot of time going over this book. They are Marc, Carol Saller, Tracy Schoenle, Jim Armstrong, and Brian Johnson.

I wrote this book for people like Harry Greenhouse. He's a great guy and a baseball fan who reminds me of me when I was his age. He likes to tell me when I'm wrong, and that helped make this book better, too.

And a big thanks to my wonderful wife, Marie, just for being there.